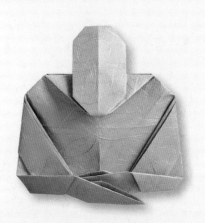

Buddhist ORIGAMI

Buddhist ORIGAMI

15 Easy-to-Make Symbols to Bring Peace, Wisdom & Harmony into Your Home

NICK ROBINSON

WATKINS PUBLISHING

LONDON

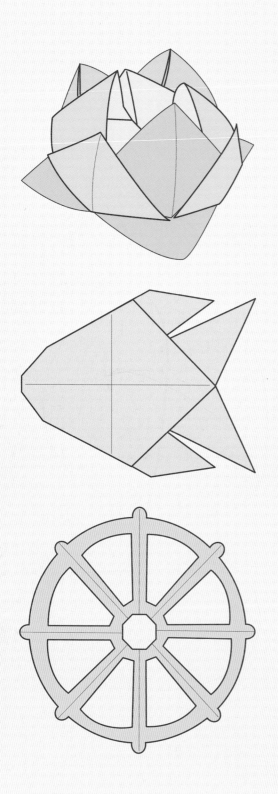

The book is dedicated to my fellow musician, Krys Zasada

Buddhist Origami
Nick Robinson

First published in the UK and USA in 2014 by
Watkins Publishing Limited
Sixth Floor
75 Wells Street
London W1T 3QH

A member of Osprey Group

Osprey Publishing Inc.
43-01 21st Street
Suite 220B, Long Island City
New York 11101

Senior Editors: Tania Ahsan and Fiona Robertson
Managing Designer: Luana Gobbo
Commissioned Photography: Jules Selmes

A CIP record for this book is available from the British Library

ISBN: 978-1-78028-637-2
10 9 8 7 6 5 4 3 2 1

Typeset in Agenda and Chaparral Pro
Colour reproduction by PDQ, UK
Printed in China

Contents

"If a man speaks or acts with a good thought, happiness follows him like a shadow that never leaves him."

THE DHAMMAPADA, 1:2

The Spirit of Origami

For many centuries origami has played a central part in traditional Japanese ceremonies of life and death, from birth rites to weddings to funerals. From the late 6th century, when paper was first introduced into Japan, Shinto priests were fascinated by the beauty, purity and perfection of this material. These qualities were attributed to the gods, so the folding of paper became symbolic of both prayer and offering.

In the West, paper has a more prosaic history, connected with the storage and distribution of knowledge rather than with any spiritual association. However, as we in the modern world look increasingly for spiritual enlightenment, the practice of origami (from *ori*, meaning "folding", and *kami*, meaning "paper") has found many adherents who believe there is more to the art than mechanical skill. They strive toward a perfection based on capturing the spirit of the subject with minimal creases, rather than a quest for technological complexity.

The late Japanese Master Akira Yoshizawa, known as the father of contemporary origami, produced clear instructions for folding some of his creations. Yet it's widely acknowledged that few people can even come close to imbuing the models he folded with the same spirit that he gave them. In his youth, Yoshizawa had studied to be a Buddhist priest. Before he folded he would pray and strive to understand the spirit of the creature he was about to create. Many folders see a link between origami

WEDDING SYMBOLISM
In Japan, a crane (opposite) is seen as a bringer of happiness; traditionally, 1,000 paper cranes are given as a wedding gift to represent 1,000 years of married bliss. An origami butterfly (below) symbolizes the bride or groom.

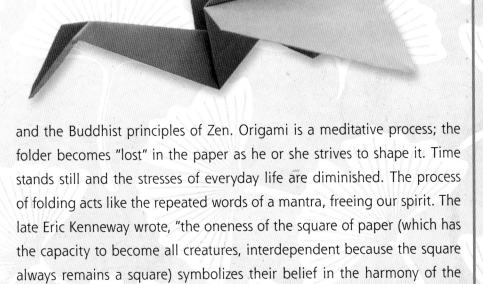

and the Buddhist principles of Zen. Origami is a meditative process; the folder becomes "lost" in the paper as he or she strives to shape it. Time stands still and the stresses of everyday life are diminished. The process of folding acts like the repeated words of a mantra, freeing our spirit. The late Eric Kenneway wrote, "the oneness of the square of paper (which has the capacity to become all creatures, interdependent because the square always remains a square) symbolizes their belief in the harmony of the universe and the presence of the Buddha-nature in all things."

An origami designer finds that each original model reaches a point where it seems "complete", when adding further folds would diminish its effectiveness. Thus designers who seek perfection question the addition of every crease – if the original square is the "purest" of states, a great model will work with the paper organically, without superfluous creases. Some believe that the model already lies dormant within the paper, simply awaiting an enlightened folder to liberate it. And so the classic origami models are discovered rather than created. When you follow the steps of this kind of design, you really feel that the artwork you are shaping is "meant to be". It is hugely satisfying to breathe life into an origami model, to give it a spirit that can be sensed by you and by others.

TIP: EXPRESSING IDEAS

In the purist origami tradition, scissors, decoration and even superfluous creases are forbidden, encouraging the folder to focus on the possibilities of the paper itself. But this eight-spoked wheel (see page 18) – a wonderful symbol of the Noble Eightfold Path contained within the wheel of the Dharma – can only be created with scissors. Don't feel constrained by origami taboos. If you are seeking inspiration, Buddhist traditions around the world can provide a rich source of decorative ideas.

The Art of Paper Folding

How to use this book

Origami is the art of making models from sheets of paper, ideally with no use of scissors or glue. A simple set of internationally accepted symbols is all you need to understand the diagrams in this book, although you will certainly need to study and practise for the more complicated designs. Some will find paper-folding easier than others, but anyone can do it with a bit of dedication.

This book is intended as a collection of beautiful models of Buddhist symbols rather than a book on origami technique. However, if you work through the designs in the suggested order, you will build up all the skills you need to tackle most origami projects. Always fold each project several times – each new version will be more refined and elegant. Some may take several attempts to get right. Buddhism is all about simplicity, so try to keep the folds as clean and precise as possible. As you shape each model into three dimensions, experiment in order to make the design your own. You are not just following a set of instructions, but imbuing the models with inner life and even something of your own state of mind.

How to fold

It's safe to say that if you rush origami, it will show in the results. So, please try to be patient at all times and to fold as slowly and neatly as you can. If possible, arrange to fold in a quiet, clean environment, with decent lighting and few distractions. The act of folding can then become a meditative state and you will feel relaxed and refreshed afterwards.

GREAT GIFT IDEAS
While there is huge satisfaction in making an origami design for its own sake, you can also use any of the models in this book (such as the frog and fish below, on pages 58 and 50) as original decorations or gifts.

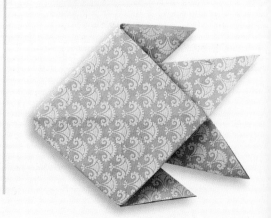

When learning a new design, fold, unfold and refold each step a few times, so you are clear what is happening and what the diagrams are trying to explain. When the model is complete, make it again at least twice – each time your results will improve. Only you can decide what standard to aim for, so be patient and set your sights high!

Following the diagrams

The instructions in this book consist of two elements – diagrams and text. While an experienced folder will not need the text very often, a beginner is encouraged to use every available hint. A suggested method could be:

- Look at the step diagram
- Read the text
- Imagine the result of the fold
- Look at the next step diagram to see how it will develop
- Make the fold, slowly and carefully

If you are keen to refine your skills, repeatedly undo and redo the fold, seeing how the paper is moving and how the diagram is trying to illustrate this. Being able to predict what each step will result in allows you to make a much more precise fold. You will improve with practice.

If you find you cannot complete a model, put it to one side and try again the next day. With complex models, it may take several attempts to achieve a decent standard. There is no shortcut to folding ability.

Think creatively at all times – if you want to depart from the given sequence to try to experiment, go for it. You can always return to the instructions later. Many creative giants began by modifying existing work.

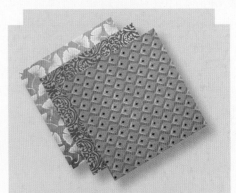

TIP: CHOOSING PAPER
Today, there is an endless range of different types of paper available. Thickness, texture and strength of fibre mean each type may suit one design but not another. You will soon learn to gauge a sheet, by folding it and feeling it. Try thick paper, try thin. You can also experiment with the many different colours and patterns on offer. When following origami diagrams, remember that the convention is to show paper with a coloured and a white side. This may, of course, not be the case in reality. The papers supplied with this book, for example, have contrasting colours and/or patterns on both sides.

Basic folds and techniques

The graphic conventions explained below allow folders to make designs even if the instruction text is in another language. This is one of the reasons why origami has such international appeal. After a while, you will need to refer to the written words only occasionally. You may find subtle differences between one book and the next, but the basic set of symbols is pretty consistent.

VALLEY FOLD   Following the arrow, make a fold away from you.

FOLD AND UNFOLD   Fold from the hollow to the solid arrowheads, then unfold

MOUNTAIN FOLD   The paper is folded behind or underneath. You can often turn the paper over and make this as a valley crease.

OPEN OUT / UNFOLD   A wide, hollow arrow is a flexible symbol and indicates paper is either pulled out or unfolded.

REPEAT STEPS   To save time and effort, any steps that are repeated are indicated by an arrow with a short line through the stem. It will tell you which steps to repeat and/or how many times to repeat a single move.

PUSH THE PAPER   A small black triangle indicates that you should press part of the paper, often to encourage a flap or point to fold slightly against its will.

ROTATE PAPER   This symbol tells you to rotate the paper in the direction of the arrows. It might indicate a 90 or 180 degree turn, or even an arbitrary amount – you judge by looking at the next step.

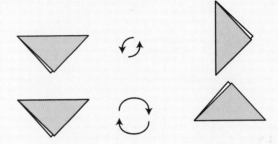

TURN THE PAPER OVER   Lift the paper up and turn it over from side to side.

OUTSIDE REVERSE FOLD   The paper is pre-creased in step 1, then wrapped outside itself in step 2, producing step 3.

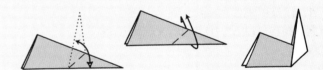

INSIDE REVERSE FOLD   The paper is folded inside other layers, so it is the opposite of the outside reverse. Here are two different applications of the move, on a point and on a corner.

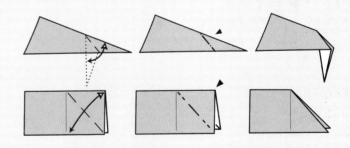

SQUASH FOLD   Generally, an edge is lifted up and squashed symmetrically in half. This move can be pre-creased (so all necessary creases are in place) or just made directly into the paper.

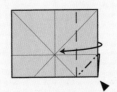
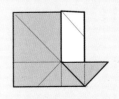

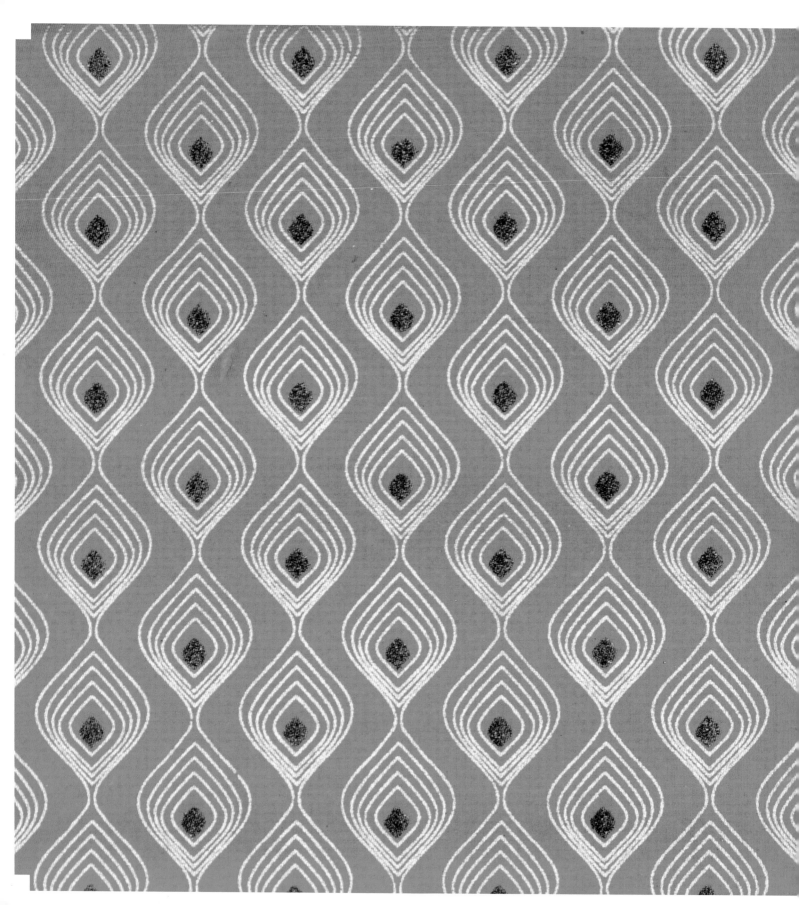

Buddhist Symbols

In this chapter you will create the famous symbols of Buddhist thought, from the eight-spoked Buddhist Wheel representing the Noble Eightfold Path to the Vase of Wealth, symbolizing spiritual abundance. Other designs, such as the Lotus of Peace and the Temple Boxes, have a simplicity and symmetry that make them perfect as objects of meditation.

Conch Shell

The conch shell is one of the best-known symbols of Buddhism, representing
the fame of the Buddha's teaching and trumpeting the truth of the Dharma.
This pretty paper shell can be placed on a home altar to remind you of
the beautiful patterns and natural symmetry of our world.

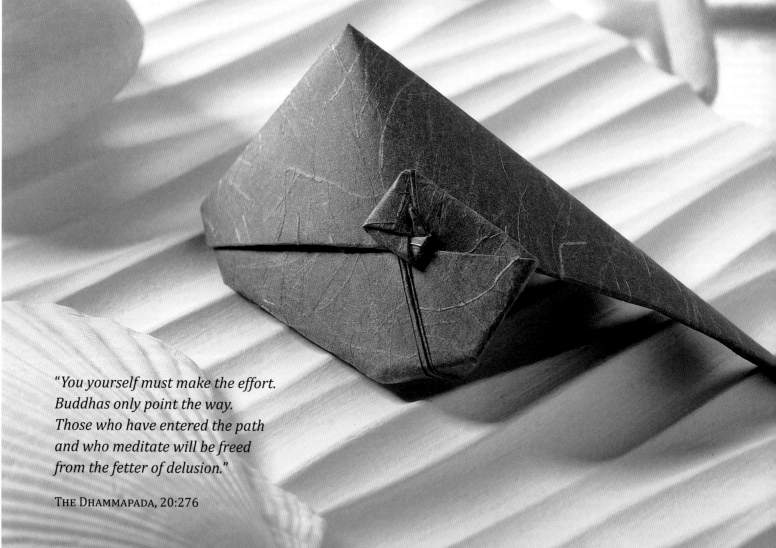

"You yourself must make the effort.
Buddhas only point the way.
Those who have entered the path
and who meditate will be freed
from the fetter of delusion."

THE DHAMMAPADA, 20:276

PAPER NEEDED: 1 square
LEVEL: simple

1 Starting with the coloured side upward, crease and unfold half a diagonal. Turn the paper over.

2 Fold both lower edges to the vertical crease.

3 Fold the upper edges in a similar way.

4 Make a crease that lies along the folded edge in the left half only. Turn the paper over.

5 Extend the vertical crease so it just reaches the crease on the right.

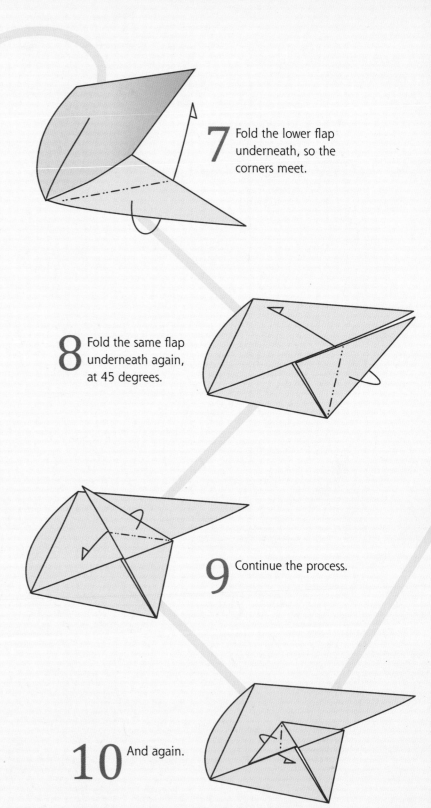

7 Fold the lower flap underneath, so the corners meet.

8 Fold the same flap underneath again, at 45 degrees.

9 Continue the process.

10 And again.

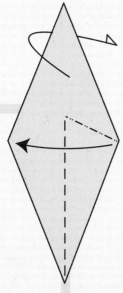

6 Fold the right corner to the left, swinging the upper half behind. The top half of the paper now becomes 3D and slightly curved.

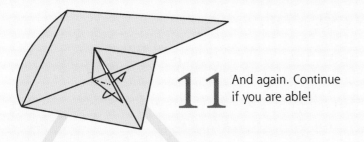

11 And again. Continue if you are able!

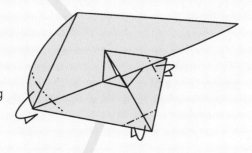

12 Now shape the model by folding corners behind.

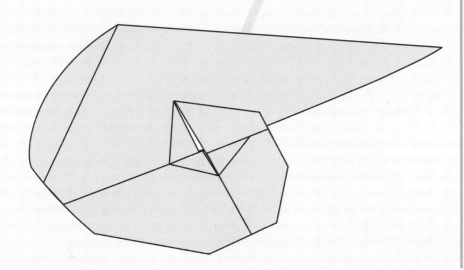

TIP: CONFIDENCE IS KEY

Once you've mastered step 6, this is a very simple design. The main issues will be aligning your folds correctly and folding with confidence. Take your time and don't worry too much about what you're doing: you will find you improve with each version you fold. Several completed shells set atop a table as if they were waterlilies on a pond look particularly dramatic. They make a great image for contemplation.

Buddhist Wheel

This design is of one of the most recognizable of Buddhist symbols: the wheel of Dharma. The eight spokes of the wheel represent the Noble Eightfold Path.

"It is the Noble Eightfold Path, the way that leads to the extinction of suffering, namely: right view, right thought, right speech, right bodily action, right livelihood, right effort, right mindfulness and right concentration."

THE SAMYUTTA NIKAYA

PAPER NEEDED: 1 square
LEVEL: simple

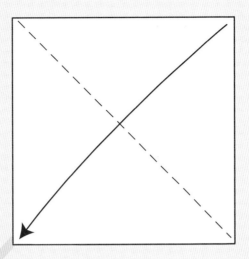

1 Start with a large, thin square, white side upward. Fold in half from top right to bottom left.

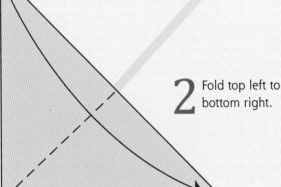

2 Fold top left to bottom right.

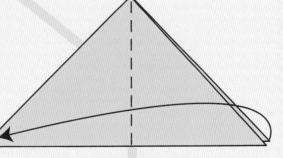

3 Fold in half (all layers) from right to left.

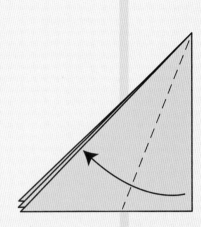

4 Fold the right vertical edge to the left (longest) edge.

5 Carefully cut out the shaded areas.

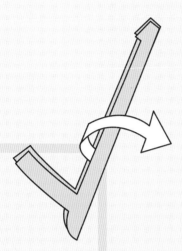

6 Unfold half the layers to the right.

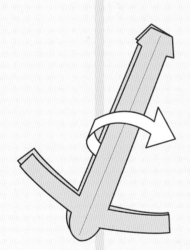

7 Unfold half the layers again.

8 Unfold again, to the left. Repeat a final time.

TIP: EXPERIMENTATION

Unlike the other designs in this book, the Buddhist Wheel requires the use of scissors – something that is frowned upon by purists, although still within the Japanese origami tradition. All the cuts in this design are suggested outlines, so feel free to experiment and see how that affects the final shape. Thin paper makes the cutting easier – try using a sheet of newspaper!

Pagoda

It is satisfying to stack up finished models to create the Pagoda; you are building a whole that is greater than its identical component parts. This is an easy shape to flatten and post – why not use it to create a wonderful and unique letter?

"The king of death cannot touch him who looks upon the world as a mirage."

THE DHAMMAPADA, 13:170

PAPER NEEDED: 1 square per level
LEVEL: simple

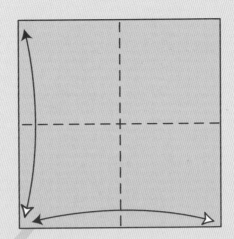

1 With the coloured side upward, crease in half and unfold, in both directions. Turn the paper over.

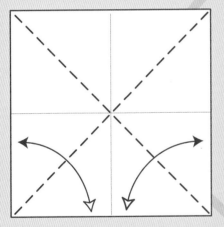

2 Crease and unfold both diagonals.

3 Collapse the paper using these creases.

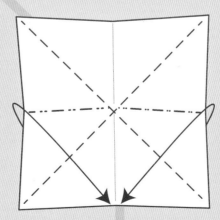

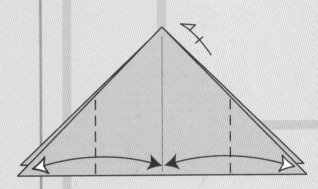

4 Fold one lower corner on each side to the centre of the lower edge, crease and unfold. Repeat underneath.

5 Fold each lower corner to the top corner. Repeat underneath.

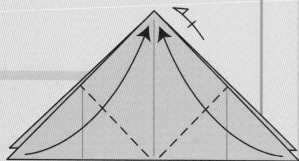

6 Open and squash the left-hand flap.

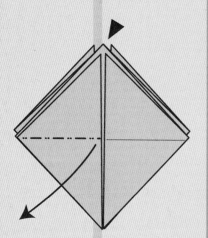

7 This is the result. Repeat on the right side and twice more underneath.

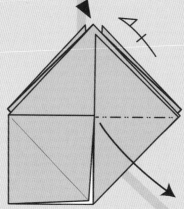

8 Fold the small squares in half. Repeat underneath.

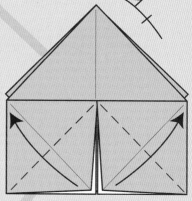

9 Swing a flap from the right to the left. Repeat underneath.

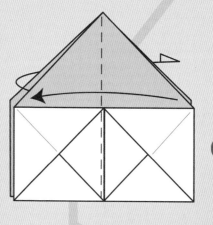

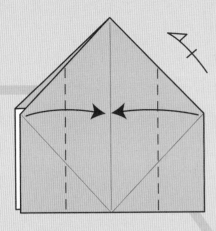

10 Fold the vertical outer edges to the centre. Repeat underneath.

11 Swing a flap from the left to the right. Repeat underneath.

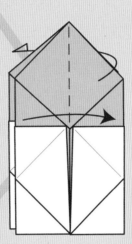

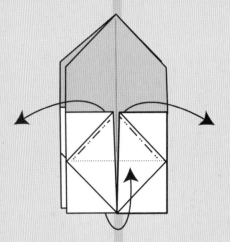

13 Fold the central corners outward, lifting the lower point as you flatten.

12 Fold the lower edge to the inner white edge, crease and unfold. Repeat underneath.

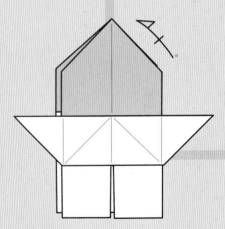

14 Repeat underneath.

15

Make several more models in the same way, then slide them into each other to form the pagoda.

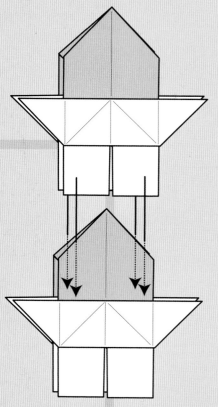

TIP: THE BIGGER PICTURE

If you use squares of decreasing size, you can give your finished pagoda an elegant taper. This is a straightforward traditional design – how high can you build it?

Lotus of Peace

This simple yet effective design is perfect for experimentation using different types of paper. The lotus's pleasing symmetry makes it ideal as an object of meditation.

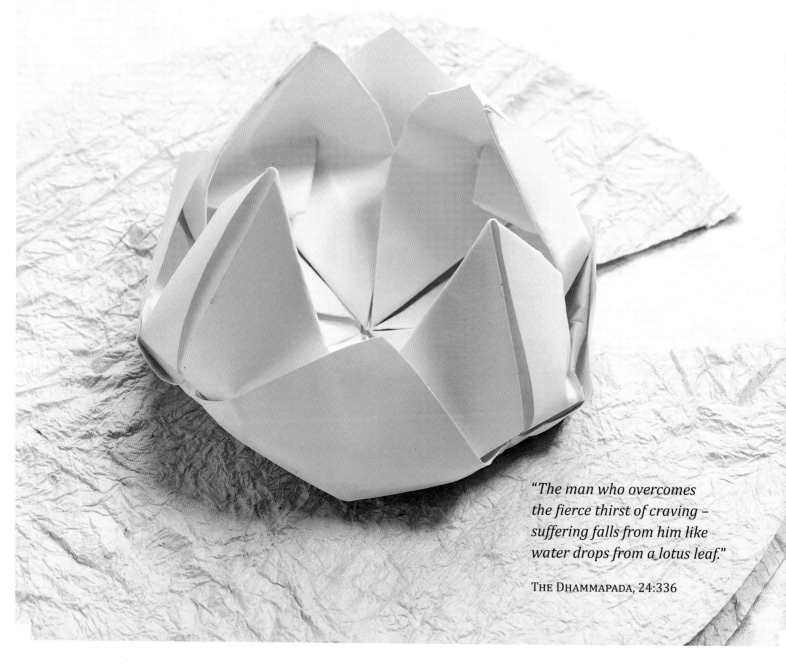

"The man who overcomes the fierce thirst of craving – suffering falls from him like water drops from a lotus leaf."

THE DHAMMAPADA, 24:336

PAPER NEEDED: 1 square
LEVEL: intermediate

1 Start with the white side upward. Crease in half, side to opposite side, in both directions.

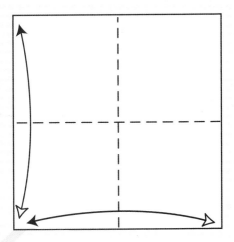

2 Fold all four corners to the centre.

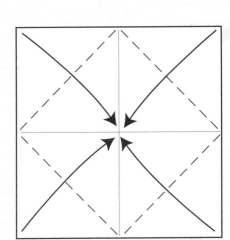

3 (Enlarged view) Again, fold all four corners to the centre. Turn the paper over.

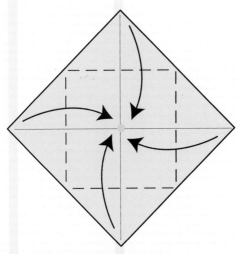

4 (Enlarged view) Fold all four corners to the centre! Fold carefully to avoid tearing the paper.

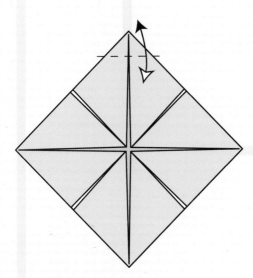

5 (Enlarged view) Fold the corner over, crease firmly and unfold.

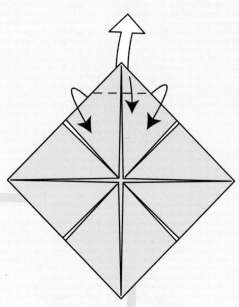

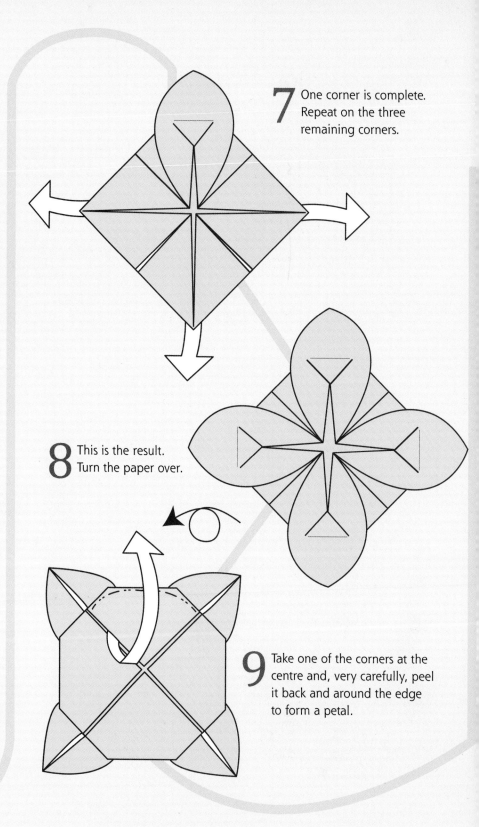

7 One corner is complete. Repeat on the three remaining corners.

6 Fold layers round from underneath, folding over the small triangular flap as you do so. It may help to unfold the layers slightly, then refold when complete.

8 This is the result. Turn the paper over.

9 Take one of the corners at the centre and, very carefully, peel it back and around the edge to form a petal.

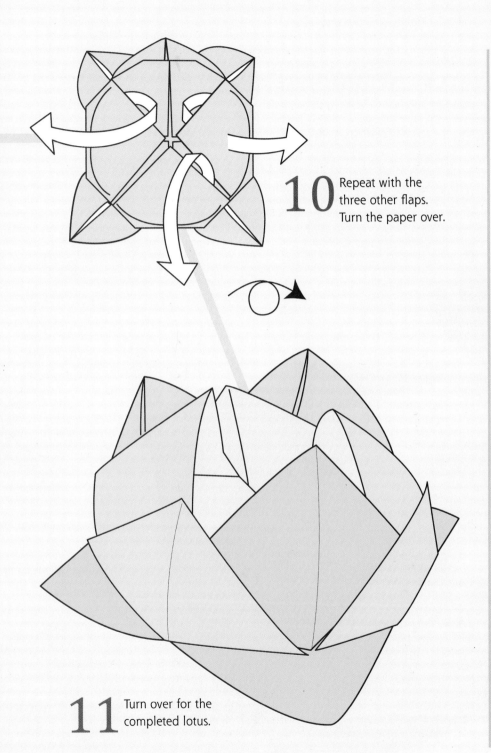

10 Repeat with the three other flaps. Turn the paper over.

11 Turn over for the completed lotus.

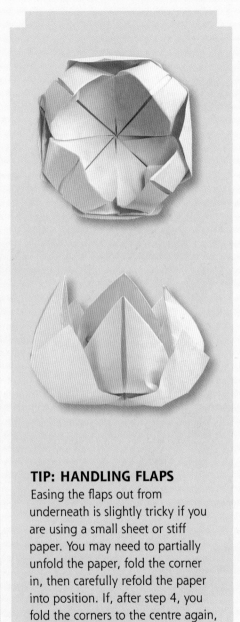

TIP: HANDLING FLAPS

Easing the flaps out from underneath is slightly tricky if you are using a small sheet or stiff paper. You may need to partially unfold the paper, fold the corner in, then carefully refold the paper into position. If, after step 4, you fold the corners to the centre again, you will have another set of flaps to pull out at the end, but the paper will become very small.

Vase of Wealth

This design is a modern variant of the clay pots used to symbolize spiritual abundance on Buddhist altars. It is not sealed at the top, so you can make paper flowers to place inside or simply contemplate the space that exists within an empty vessel.

"Be content with simple things and be free from the craving for worldly possessions."

TRADITIONAL TIBETAN TEACHING

PAPER NEEDED: 1 square
LEVEL: intermediate

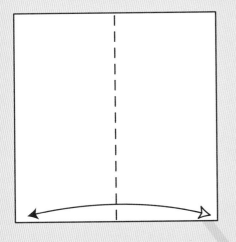

1 Start with the white side upward. Fold in half from side to side, crease and unfold.

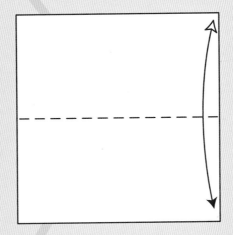

2 Fold in half in the other direction.

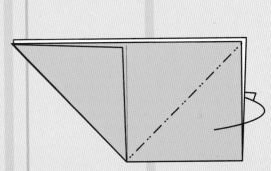

4 Fold the lower right corner behind in a similar way.

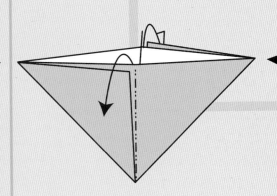

3 Fold the lower left corner to the centre of the upper edge.

5 Open the layers evenly and squash the paper open into a square.

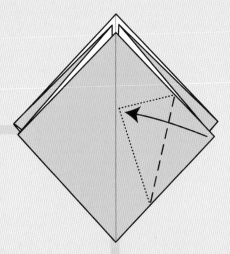

6 Fold the corner on the right to lie on the central crease, just above the centre.

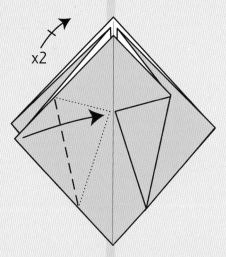

x2

7 Fold the corner on the left in to the same place. Repeat twice underneath.

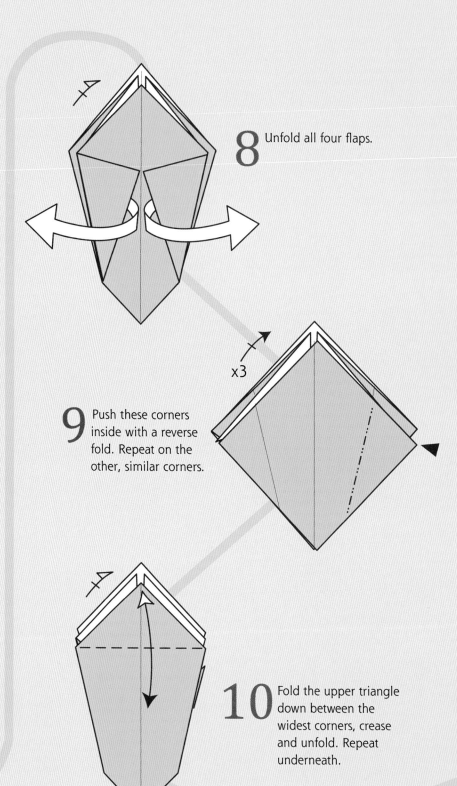

8 Unfold all four flaps.

9 Push these corners inside with a reverse fold. Repeat on the other, similar corners.

x3

10 Fold the upper triangle down between the widest corners, crease and unfold. Repeat underneath.

11 Fold one layer from right to left. Repeat underneath.

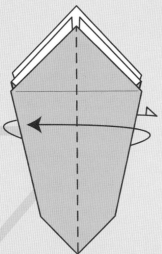

12 Repeat step 8.

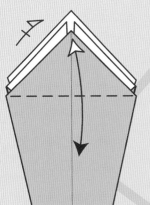

13 Fold a flap inside.

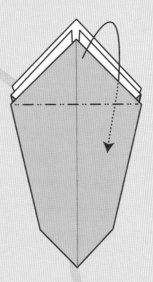

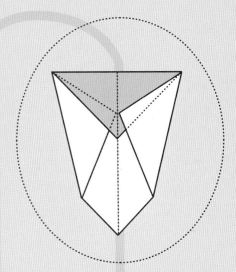

14 Here is how the flap should lie on the inside – over one internal flap, under the other.

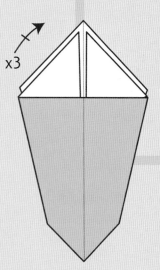

x3

15 Repeat the move on the other three flaps. You need to rearrange layers to do this as you did in step 9.

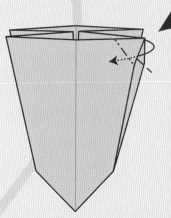

17 Reverse the corner inside, being careful to prevent other layers from opening or unfolding.

14–15 x3

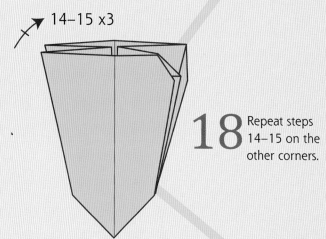

18 Repeat steps 14–15 on the other corners.

x3

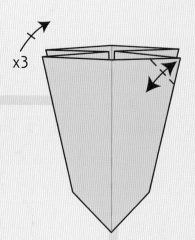

16 Fold the tip of the corner over, creasing sharply, then unfold. Repeat on the three other corners.

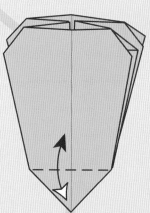

19 Fold the lower corner up where the angle changes, crease and unfold.

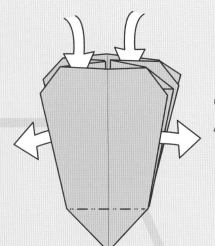

20 Put your finger inside the model and carefully ease open all the sides. The lower point opens to form the base. Shape to make it symmetrical.

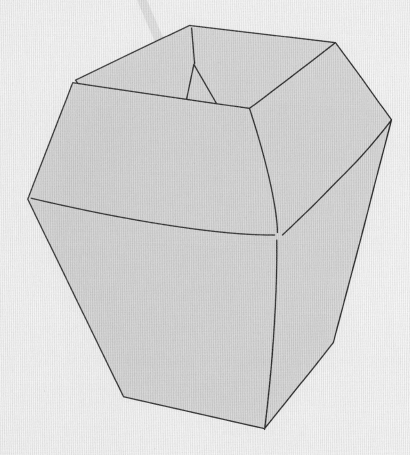

TIP: A SOLID STRUCTURE

Steps 15 and 16 are key to a solid top section – try to hold all layers and corners in place while flattening. This makes the final opening easier, but you still need to be gentle during the last step. This design is by Saburo Kase, a blind Japanese folder who has taught origami around the world for many years, assessing and correcting his students' models by touch alone.

Temple Boxes

Try to make these boxes in a state of mindfulness. When you have completed a few, string them together and hang them from a window frame. They will move in the breeze, reminding you of the tranquil state of mind in which you made them.

"It is good to apply yourself diligently to the task in hand. Intoxicated by that task, you should be completely focused, like someone striving to win a game."

FROM THE BODHICARYAVATARA
OF SHANTIDEVA

PAPER NEEDED: 1 square per box
LEVEL: complex

1 Start with the white side upward. Fold in half from side to side, crease and unfold.

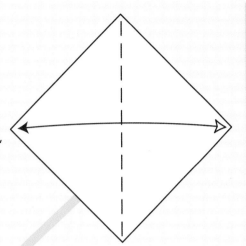

2 Fold in half upward.

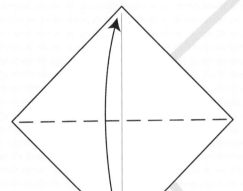

3 Fold left and right corners to the centre of the lower edge.

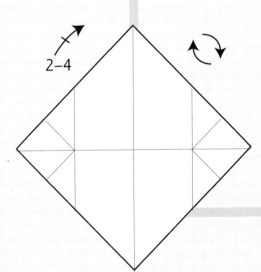

4 Fold both small triangles in half, then unfold to step 1.

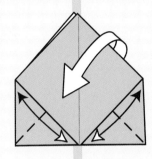

2–4

5 Repeat steps 2–4 on the other diagonal, then open again. Rotate the paper 45 degrees.

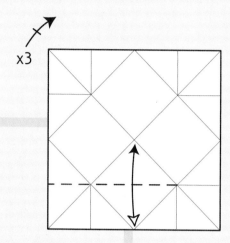

6 Extend an existing crease so that it is a valley fold where shown. Repeat on three other sides.

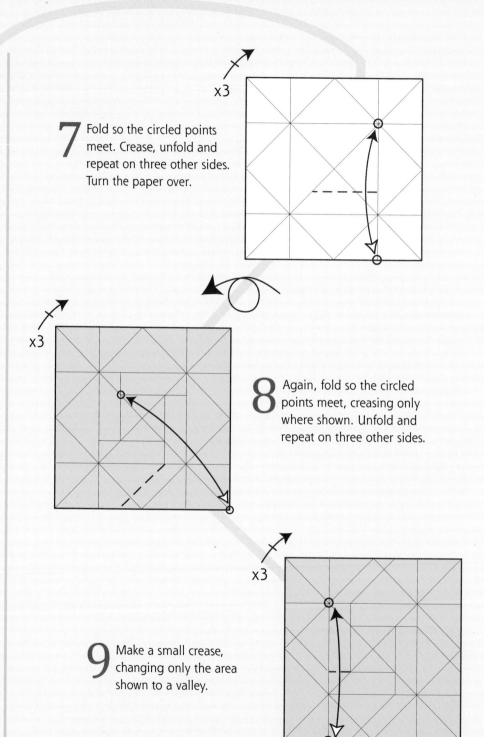

7 Fold so the circled points meet. Crease, unfold and repeat on three other sides. Turn the paper over.

8 Again, fold so the circled points meet, creasing only where shown. Unfold and repeat on three other sides.

9 Make a small crease, changing only the area shown to a valley.

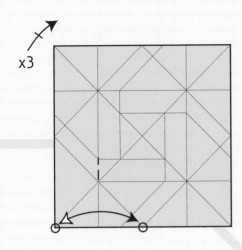

x3

10
Make a small crease, changing only the area shown to a valley.

11
Now comes the fun! All these creases should be in place. Start to form them partially all round the model, creating a small, flat, central square.

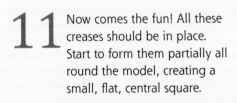

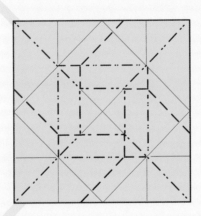

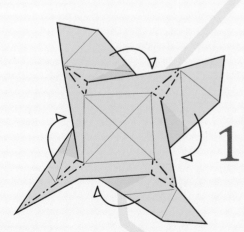

12
The pointed flaps at each corner swing to the left, twisting into position. Check the next two diagrams to see what you are aiming for.

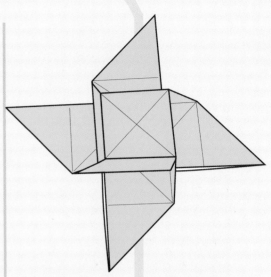

13
This is how the model should look. Turn the paper over.

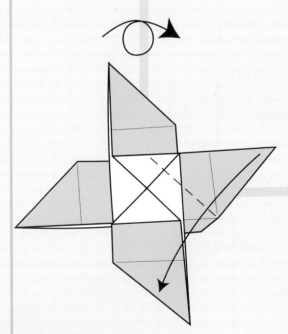

14
Fold a flap over on an existing crease.

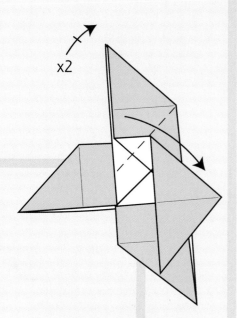

x2

15 Now fold the next flap in an anti-clockwise direction, followed by the other two flaps.

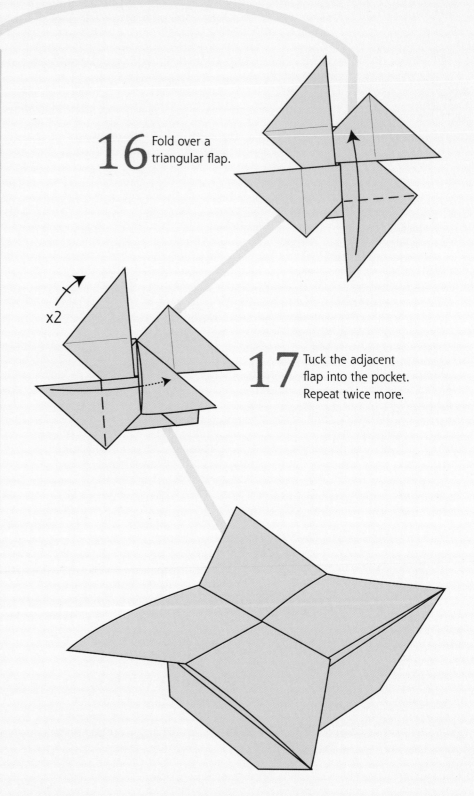

16 Fold over a triangular flap.

x2

17 Tuck the adjacent flap into the pocket. Repeat twice more.

TIP: PRECISE PRE-CREASING

Careful pre-creasing makes the final assembly
easier. If you struggle with step 12, look again
at step 11 and make sure every crease is as it
should be. Never force the paper into shape
and be careful not to add any new creases.
When you manage step 12, unfold and refold
again so that you understand how it works.

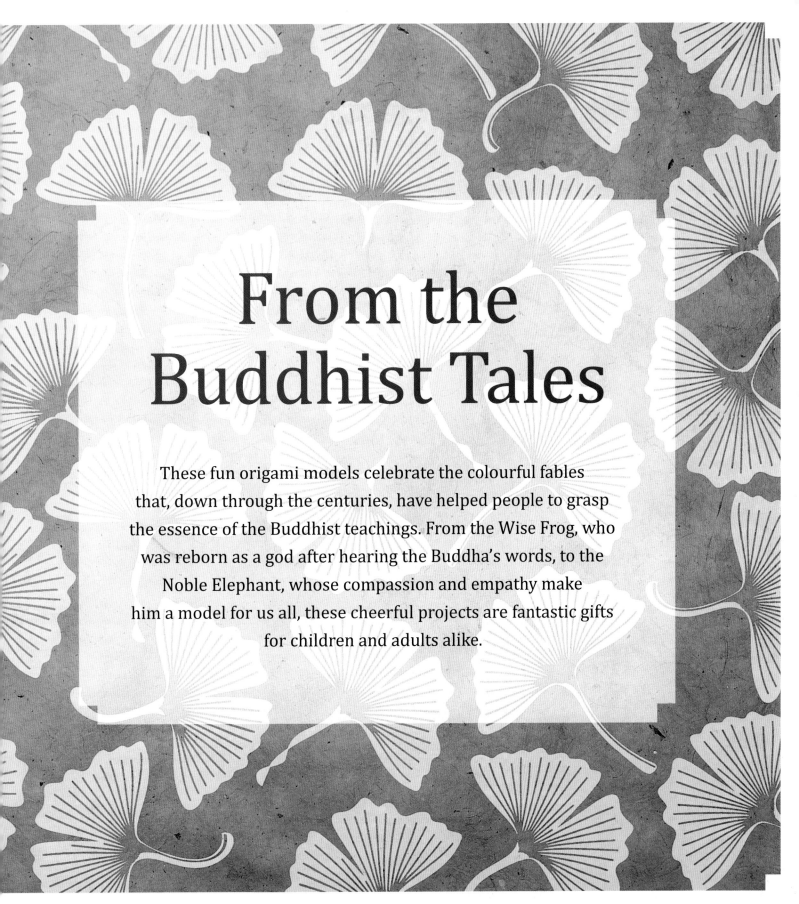

From the Buddhist Tales

These fun origami models celebrate the colourful fables
that, down through the centuries, have helped people to grasp
the essence of the Buddhist teachings. From the Wise Frog, who
was reborn as a god after hearing the Buddha's words, to the
Noble Elephant, whose compassion and empathy make
him a model for us all, these cheerful projects are fantastic gifts
for children and adults alike.

Golden Bowl

From the Jataka Tales comes the story of a beautiful golden bowl and two merchants, one greedy and the other wise. When the mean trader attempts to get the bowl by deception, the wise, compassionate one is given it at a fraction of its value as a reward for his honesty. The moral of the story is to live a life free from greed and anger.

"Let a man overcome anger by love, let him overcome evil by good; let him overcome the greedy by liberality, the liar by truth!"

THE DHAMMAPADA, 17:223

PAPER NEEDED: 1 square
LEVEL: simple

1 Start with the coloured side upward. Crease and unfold both diagonals.

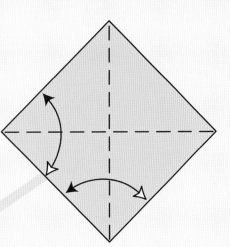

2 Fold the lower left edge to the diagonal, crease and unfold. Rotate the paper clockwise.

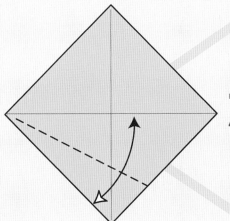

3 Repeat the last step and then repeat on the other two sides.

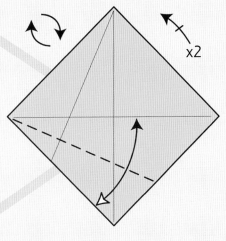

4 Make the same fold from the lower right edge, repeating all round. Turn the paper over.

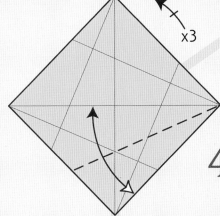

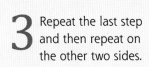

5 Fold one end of the crease to the other, so the circled points meet. Crease only in the lower section, then unfold. Rotate the paper, repeating three more times.

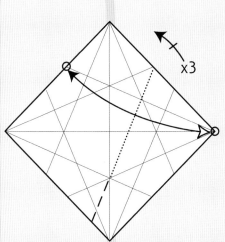

6 Fold the lower corner to the circled point, creasing only in the central section. Rotate the paper, repeating three more times.

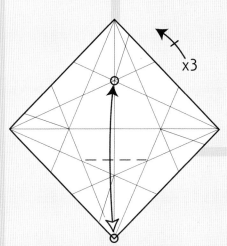

7 Fold the circled points together, creasing across the paper, then unfold.

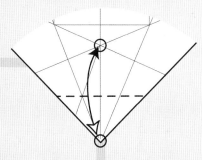

8 Fold the section shown to change into a valley fold.

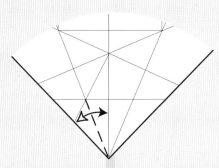

9 Fold the lower right edge to the horizontal crease. Crease, then unfold. Repeat steps 7–9 on the three other corners.

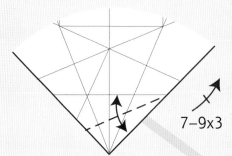

7–9x3

10 Pinch together the three mountain folds to form a small peak and push the tip downward. Then swing the flap to the left using the valley fold.

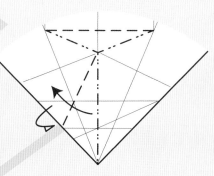

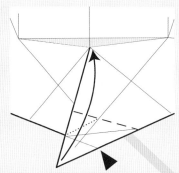

11 Fold in the corner, making a valley fold on the internal (dotted) crease.

12 Fold the flap behind on an existing crease.

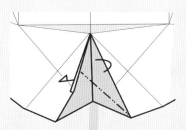

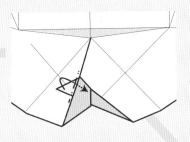

13 Tuck the small triangular flap behind to lock the layers together.

14 The corner is complete. Repeat steps 10–13 on the three remaining corners.

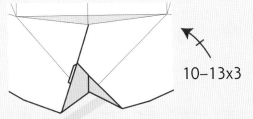

10–13x3

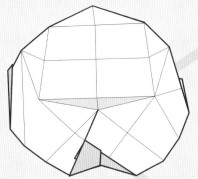

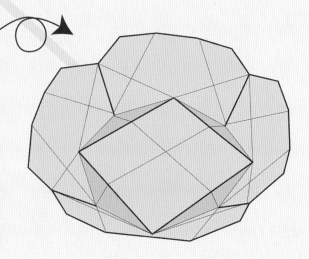

TIP: THE RIGHT PAPER

The key to a good result is to use crisp paper and make every fold clean and accurate. This design uses a pre-crease method, in which every crease you will need is made into the open square, then the folds come together at the end – surely fitting for a Buddhist design.

Fish of Harmony

In the Jataka tale called "The Empty Lake", a fish king prays to the King of Thunder and the Queen of Rain to restore balance and harmony to his drying lake. His humility and forbearance ensure that his prayers are answered – and the lake never empties again.

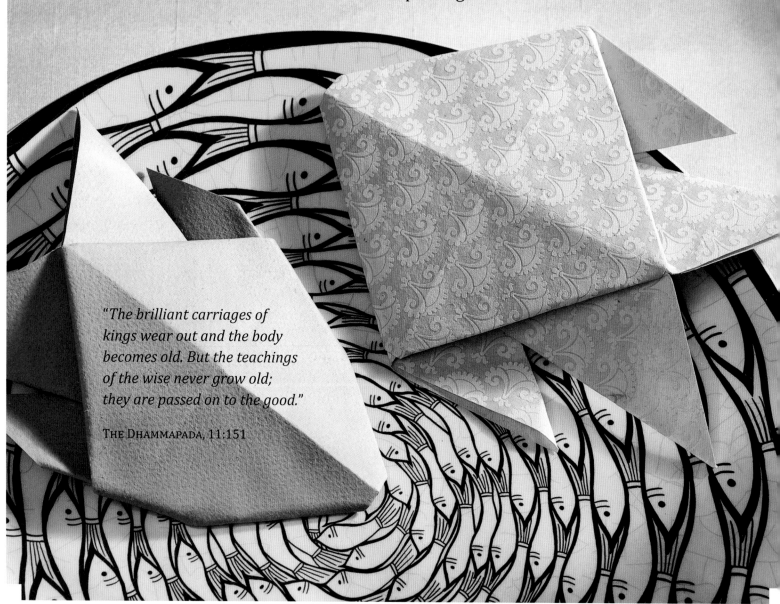

"The brilliant carriages of kings wear out and the body becomes old. But the teachings of the wise never grow old; they are passed on to the good."

THE DHAMMAPADA, 11:151

PAPER NEEDED: 1 square
LEVEL: simple

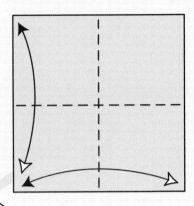

1 With the coloured side upward, crease in half and unfold, in both directions. Turn the paper over.

2 Fold upper and lower edges to the horizontal centre.

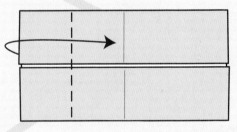

3 Fold the left edge to the vertical centre.

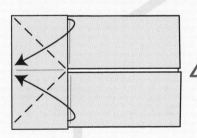

4 Fold the two corners to the centre of the left edge.

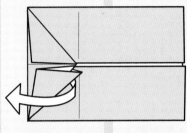

5 Carefully ease out a layer of paper and flatten it.

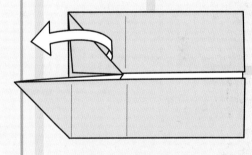

6 Repeat the last move on the upper flap.

7 Repeat steps 3–6 on the right side of the paper.

3–6

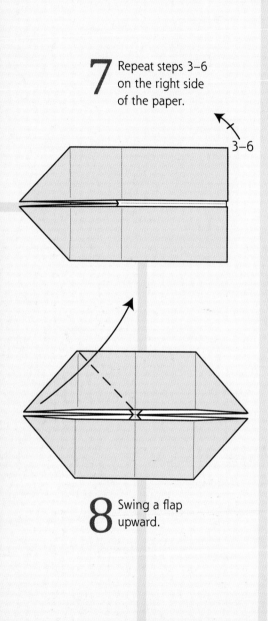

8 Swing a flap upward.

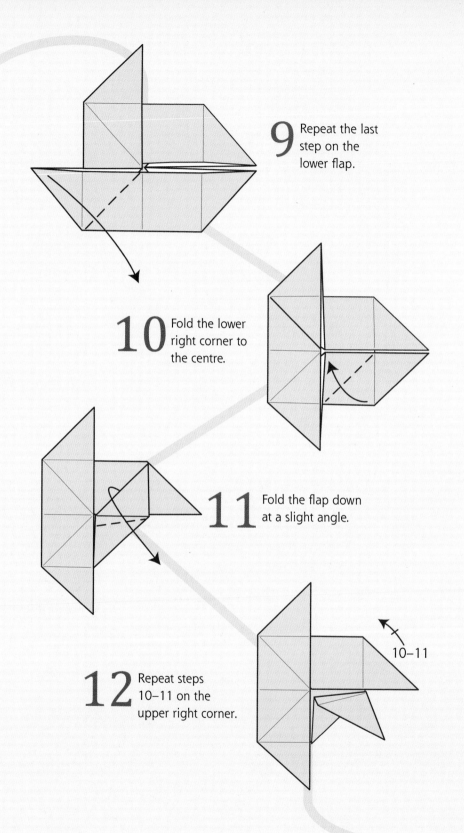

9 Repeat the last step on the lower flap.

10 Fold the lower right corner to the centre.

11 Fold the flap down at a slight angle.

10–11

12 Repeat steps 10–11 on the upper right corner.

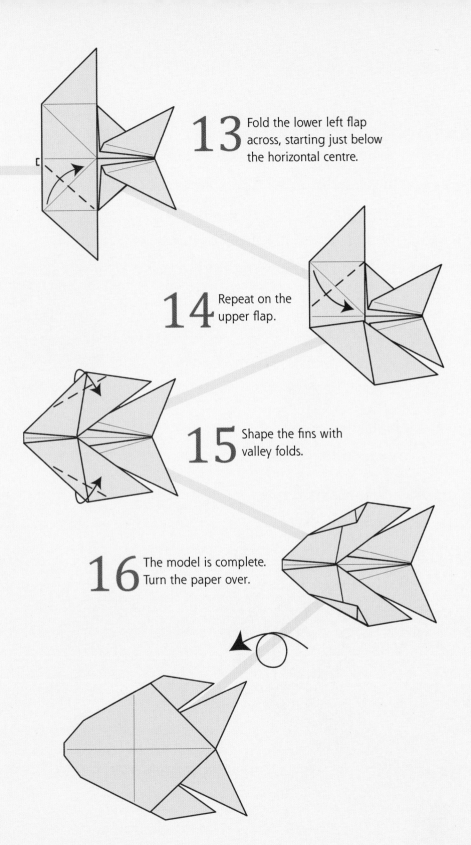

13 Fold the lower left flap across, starting just below the horizontal centre.

14 Repeat on the upper flap.

15 Shape the fins with valley folds.

16 The model is complete. Turn the paper over.

TIP: EXPRESS YOUR VISION

This design uses a multiform base, often used in origami as a basis for many different models (see Contemplating the Turtle, page 70). Feel free to adjust step 11, which determines the angle of the tail fin, or any other folds after step 11, to express how *you* think a fish should look!

Foolish Monkey

The Makkata Sutta scripture tells of the foolishness of those monkeys who stray outside their domain and are caught in the trap of hunters. The metaphor reminds the seeker that one's own domain is the realm of mindfulness.

"Look at this glittering world, like a royal carriage; the foolish are taken up by it, but the wise do not cling to it."

THE DHAMMAPADA, 13:171

PAPER NEEDED: 1 square
LEVEL: intermediate

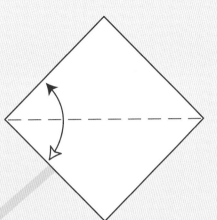

1 Start with the white side upward. Crease and unfold a diagonal.

2 Fold both right-hand edges to lie on the crease.

3 Fold the white outer edges to the same crease.

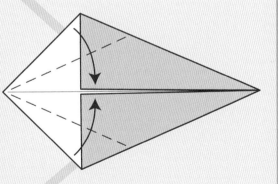

4 Fold the edges to the centre in the left section of the paper only.

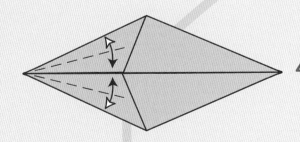

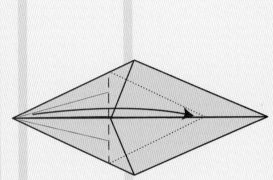

5 Fold the left flap to the right. The crease passes through the point where the folded edges meet.

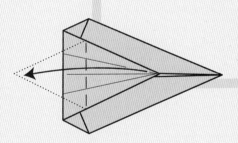

6 Fold the flap back to meet the dotted line.

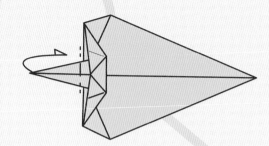

9 Fold the narrow point underneath.

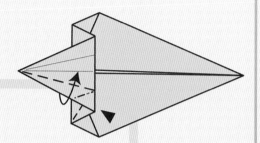

7 Fold the edge of the narrow flap to the horizontal centre, carefully squashing the paper so it will lie flat.

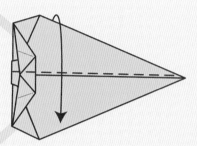

10 Fold the model in half downward.

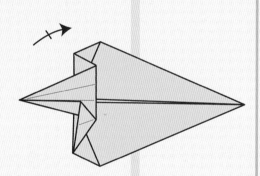

8 Repeat the last step on the upper half.

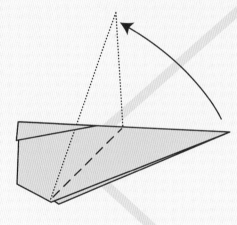

11 Fold the right hand flap upward to match the dotted line.

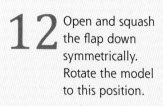

12 Open and squash the flap down symmetrically. Rotate the model to this position.

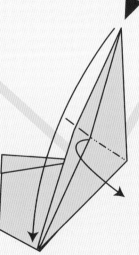

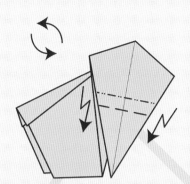

13 Make a pleat to form the face.

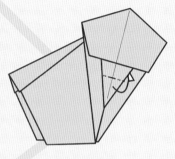

14 Fold the tip of the flap underneath

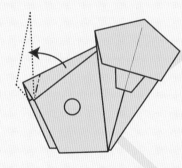

15 Hold the paper where circled and carefully pull the tail out to the dotted position. Flatten the base of the tail so it stays in place.

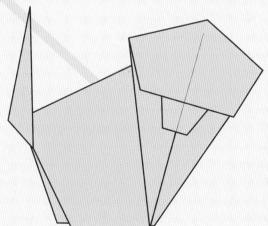

TIP: THINK "MONKEY"
Try to have a clear mental image of what you are trying to achieve. You can influence the design at various points. Squashing the corners at step 7 may seem strange, but this is a common method for narrowing a flap to form a beak or a tail. Steps 13 and 14 can be altered depending on how you want the head to look.

Wise Frog

One Buddhist tale tells of a frog who was attracted to the Buddha's voice as he taught the Dharma. While listening the frog was accidentally killed, but the potency of even momentarily hearing the truth from the Buddha allowed him to be reborn as a god.

"Your suffering is my suffering and your happiness is my happiness."

TRADITIONAL SAYING OF THE BUDDHA

PAPER NEEDED: 1 square
LEVEL: intermediate

1 Start with the white side upward. Crease in half, then unfold.

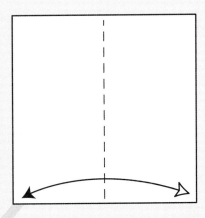

2 Fold the lower right corner to lie on the vertical crease, with the crease starting on the lower left corner.

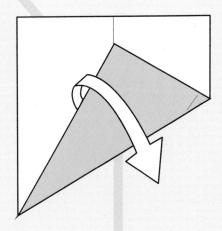

3 This is the result. Unfold the flap.

4 Repeat steps 2–3 starting at the lower right corner.

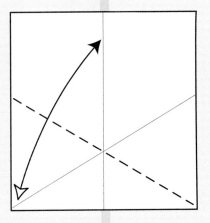

5 Fold so the circled points meet, then unfold. Repeat from the lower left corner.

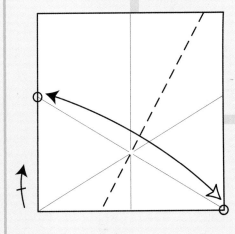

6 Put in the folds shown (changing two into mountain creases) to collapse the paper upward.

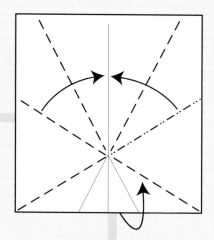

8 Fold the flap back to the left. Repeat steps 7–8 on the other side.

7–8

9 Fold the lower, white, raw edge to meet the coloured edge, squashing and re-arranging the upper flaps of paper to allow this (see the next diagram). Repeat on the other side.

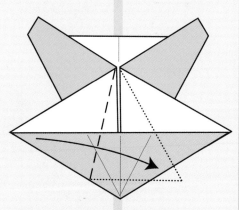

7 Fold the left flap to meet the dotted line.

10 Fold the lower part of the leg underneath, extending the crease on the dotted line to the lower left corner. Repeat on the other side.

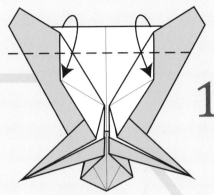

11 Fold the top edge down about one third of the way to the dotted line.

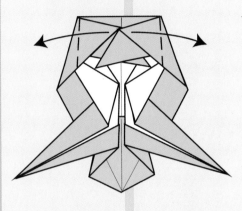

14 Fold part of both legs back out again.

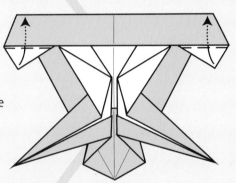

12 Tuck the white corners under the coloured layer.

15 Open out the legs fully.

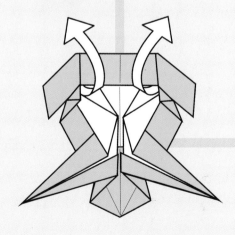

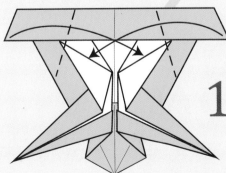

13 Fold over both rear legs – they will overlap slightly.

17 Fold part of the vertical white edge to the coloured edge, crease firmly, then unfold back to the previous step.

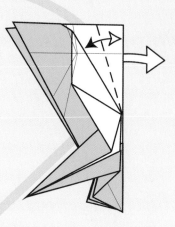

16 Mountain-fold the right half of the model behind.

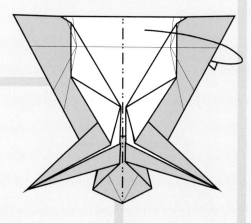

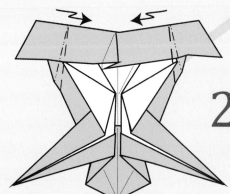

18 Pushing in the centre of the paper, form the paper into 3D with these two creases.

19 Refold the upper edge inward.

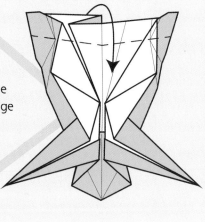

20 Reform and shape the legs.

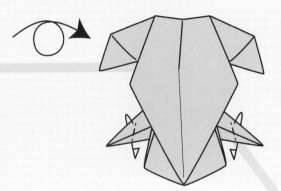

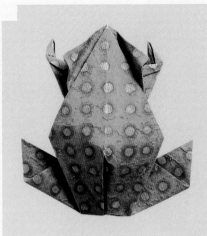

21 Fold the front legs under so they point forward.

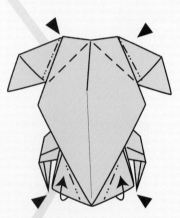

22 Shape the back of the body – make gentle creases. Lift up the sides of the head and partially squash them open to form the eyes.

TIP: BUILD UP YOUR SKILLS

This is one of the more challenging designs in the book, so try the simpler projects before attempting it. Step 9 may seem awkward, but once you have mastered it, the rest of the design should prove easier. Steps 20–23 are open to interpretation. Use your own judgement and try to capture the true essence of a frog!

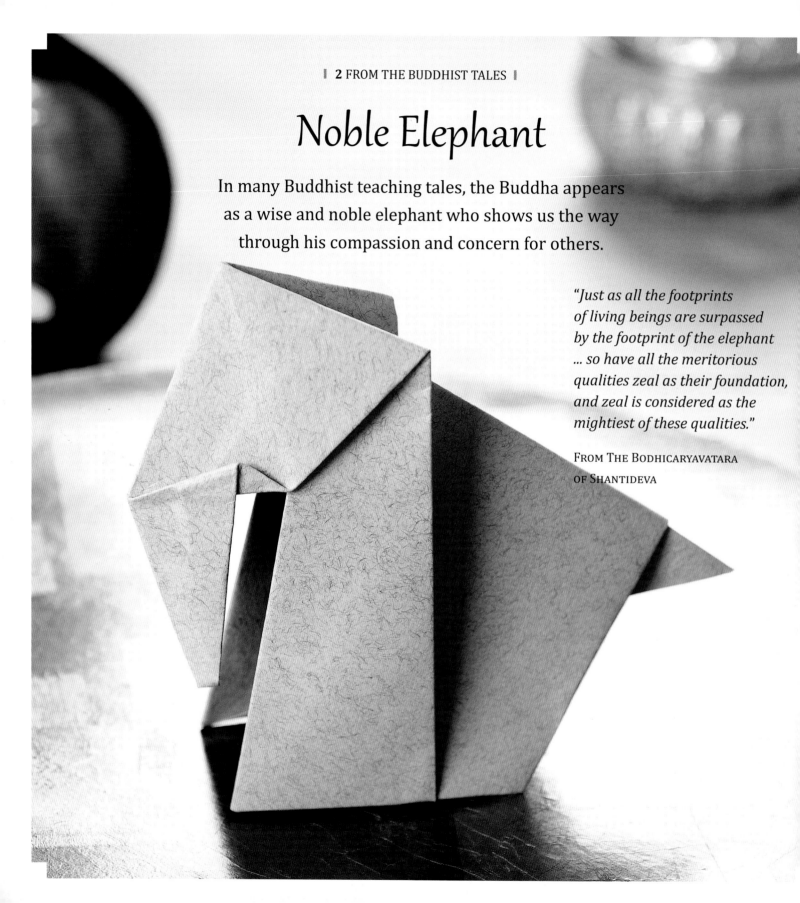

Noble Elephant

In many Buddhist teaching tales, the Buddha appears as a wise and noble elephant who shows us the way through his compassion and concern for others.

"Just as all the footprints of living beings are surpassed by the footprint of the elephant ... so have all the meritorious qualities zeal as their foundation, and zeal is considered as the mightiest of these qualities."

FROM THE BODHICARYAVATARA OF SHANTIDEVA

PAPER NEEDED: 1 square
LEVEL: intermediate

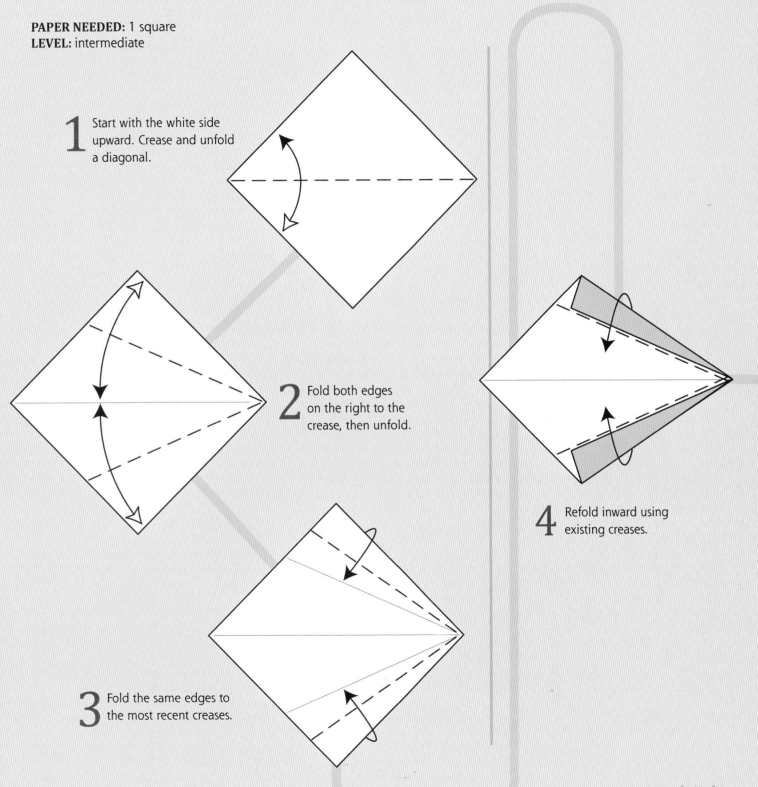

1 Start with the white side upward. Crease and unfold a diagonal.

2 Fold both edges on the right to the crease, then unfold.

3 Fold the same edges to the most recent creases.

4 Refold inward using existing creases.

5 Fold the right corner to roughly where the (imaginary) dotted line lies. Turn the paper over.

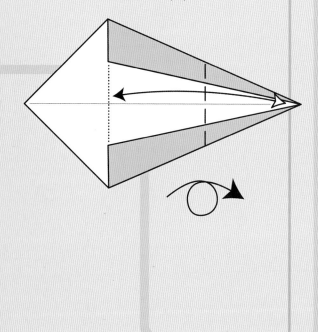

6 Make a crease between the lower corner and the intersection of creases only. Let a coloured flap flip out from underneath. See the next diagram.

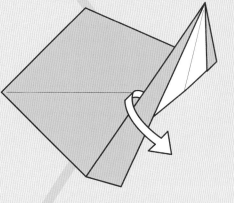

7 This is the result. Unfold the last step.

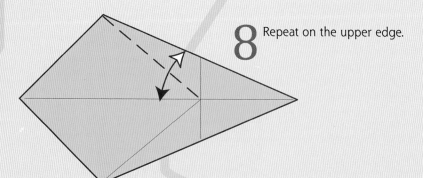

8 Repeat on the upper edge.

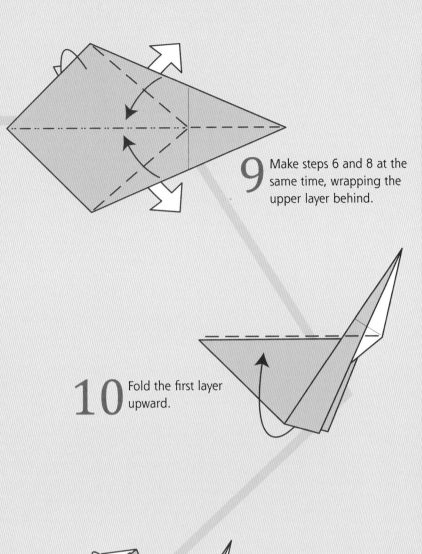

9 Make steps 6 and 8 at the same time, wrapping the upper layer behind.

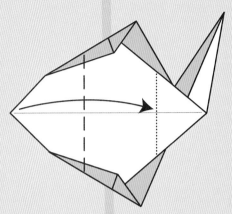

12 Fold the left corner to roughly where the (imaginary) dotted line lies.

10 Fold the first layer upward.

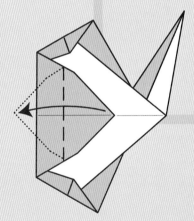

13 Fold the same corner back out to form the tail.

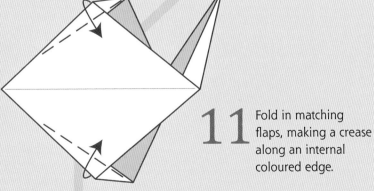

11 Fold in matching flaps, making a crease along an internal coloured edge.

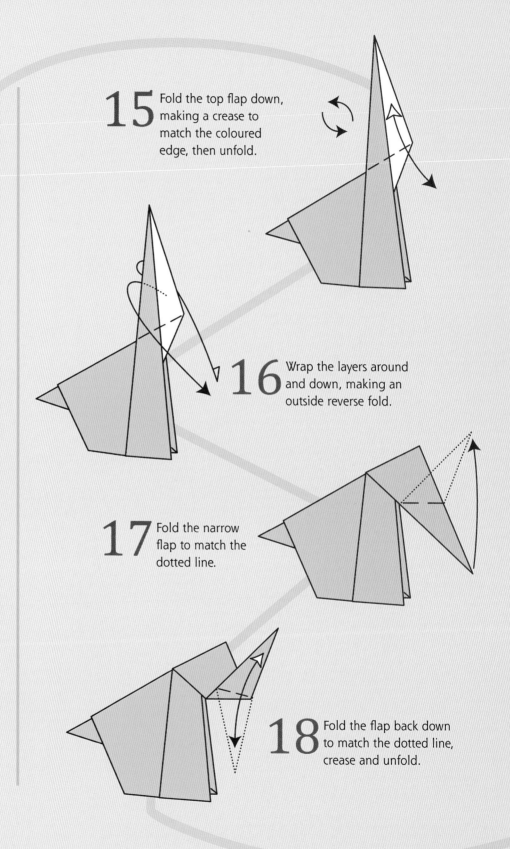

15 Fold the top flap down, making a crease to match the coloured edge, then unfold.

16 Wrap the layers around and down, making an outside reverse fold.

17 Fold the narrow flap to match the dotted line.

18 Fold the flap back down to match the dotted line, crease and unfold.

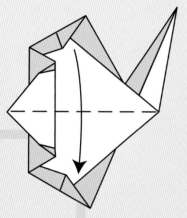

14 Fold in half downward. Rotate the paper.

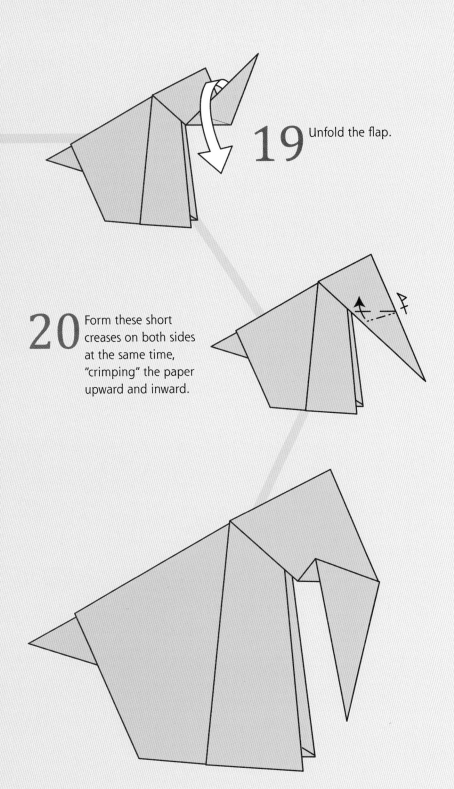

19 Unfold the flap.

20 Form these short creases on both sides at the same time, "crimping" the paper upward and inward.

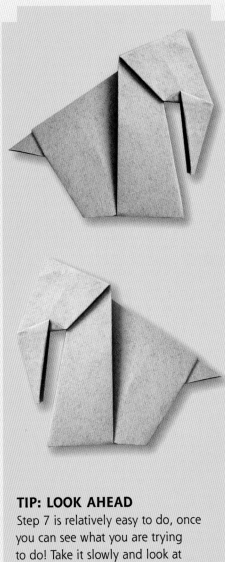

TIP: LOOK AHEAD

Step 7 is relatively easy to do, once you can see what you are trying to do! Take it slowly and look at the diagram of the next step for guidance. Step 20 is an origami "crimp"; simply repeat the crease shown on the underside at the same time.

Contemplating the Turtle

Two geese flying home asked their very good friend, a turtle, to come with them.
The only way the turtle could come was by clamping his mouth onto a stick
that the geese carried between them. When some children mocked him,
the turtle opened his mouth to rebuke them – and fell to his death.
Wisdom is in seeing where your true benefit lies.

*"Let a man overcome hatred
and pride and all fetters.
He who does not cling to name
or form, and who calls nothing
his own, will not be destroyed
by sorrow."*

THE DHAMMAPADA, 17:221

PAPER NEEDED: 1 square
LEVEL: simple

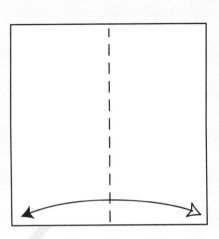

1 Start with the white side upward. Fold in half from side to side, crease and unfold.

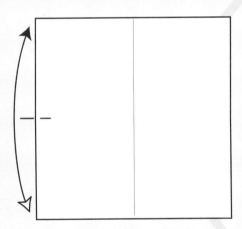

2 Fold the two corners to meet, but only make a small pinch before unfolding.

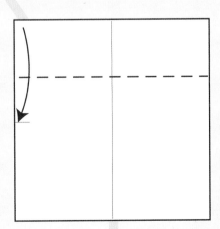

3 Fold the upper edge to the pinch-mark.

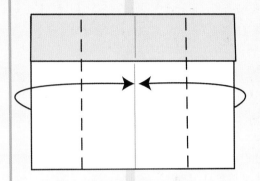

4 Fold the left and right edges to the vertical centre.

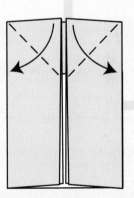

5 Fold the upper (inside) corners to meet the outer edges.

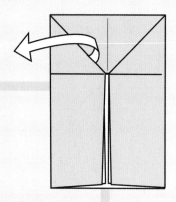

6 Ease out the first layer of paper on the left side.

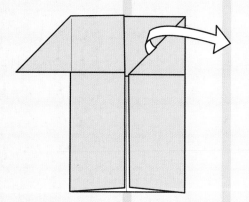

7 Repeat on the right side.

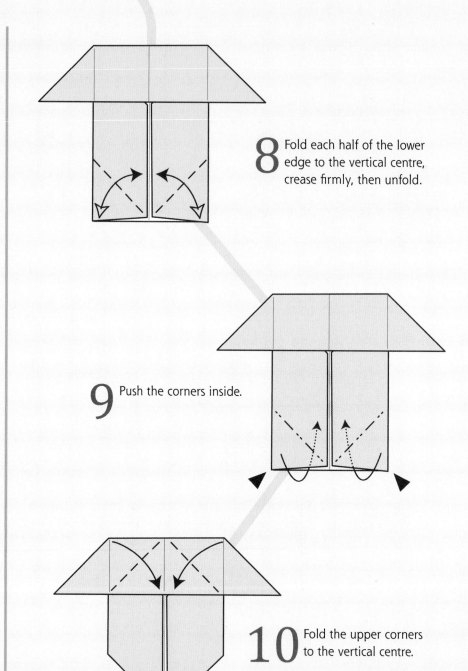

8 Fold each half of the lower edge to the vertical centre, crease firmly, then unfold.

9 Push the corners inside.

10 Fold the upper corners to the vertical centre.

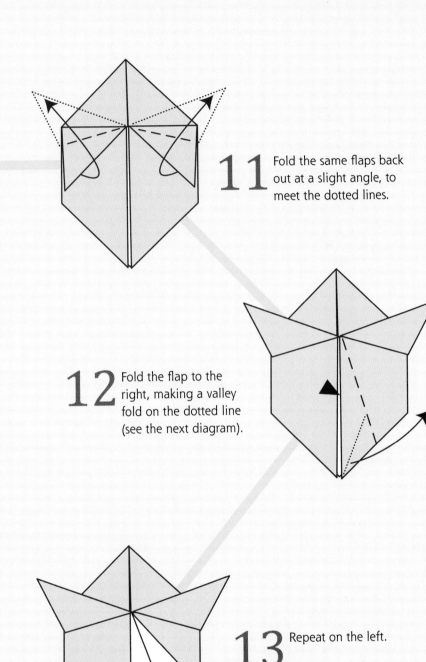

11 Fold the same flaps back out at a slight angle, to meet the dotted lines.

12 Fold the flap to the right, making a valley fold on the dotted line (see the next diagram).

13 Repeat on the left.

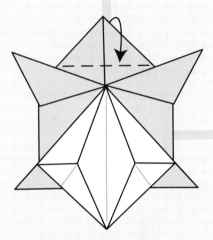

14 Fold the top triangle downward.

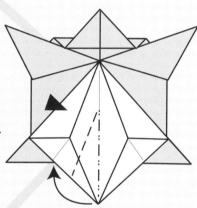

16 Make a valley crease at an angle to the vertical.

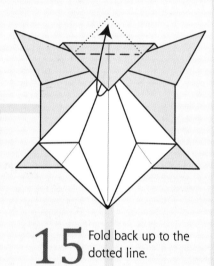

15 Fold back up to the dotted line.

17 Use the last crease to make an angled pleat, forming the paper into 3D in the shape of a bowl.

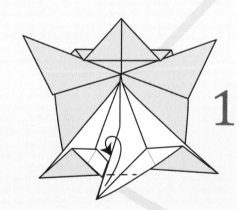

18 Fold the lower flap upward and tuck the end behind a flap to secure it.

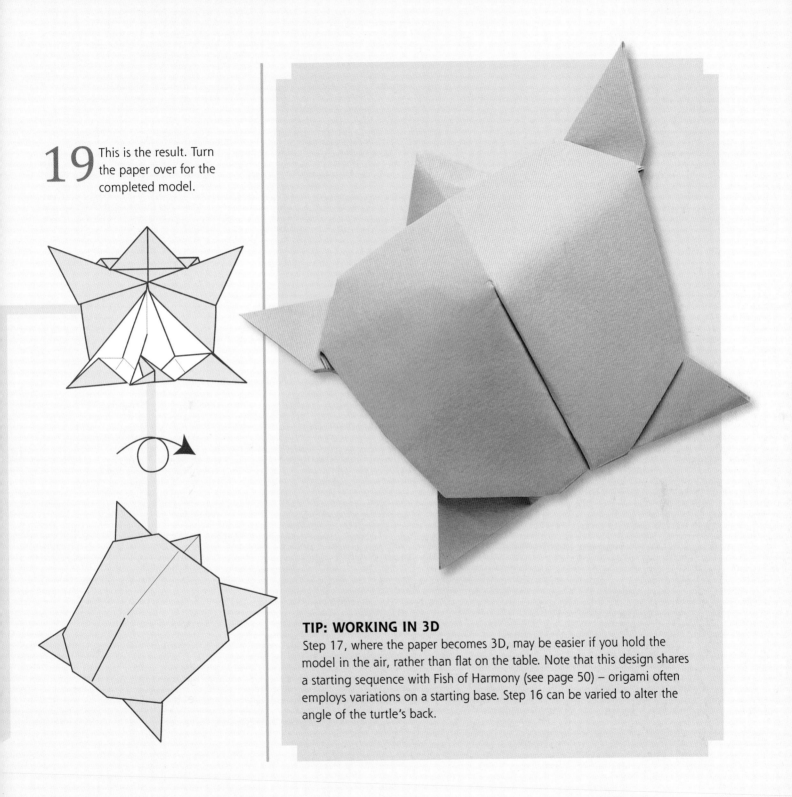

19 This is the result. Turn the paper over for the completed model.

TIP: WORKING IN 3D

Step 17, where the paper becomes 3D, may be easier if you hold the model in the air, rather than flat on the table. Note that this design shares a starting sequence with Fish of Harmony (see page 50) – origami often employs variations on a starting base. Step 16 can be varied to alter the angle of the turtle's back.

Images of the Buddha

This chapter contains two of this book's most challenging projects: the Seated Buddha and the Meditating Buddha. It is fitting that these beautiful models of the Buddha should be attempted only after you have explored the other projects; in this way you will acquire the techniques of origami as you journey through the ideas of Buddhism. But first try making the simple Desk Buddha, who will help you focus on your folding!

Desk Buddha

Having this Buddha on your desk will remind you to stay focused and calm. It is a friendly symbol of the heightened level of mindful awareness you achieve when you apply yourself in a singular way to the task at hand.

"Without knowledge there is no meditation; without meditation there is no knowledge. He who has knowledge and meditation nears nirvana."

THE DHAMMAPADA, 25:372

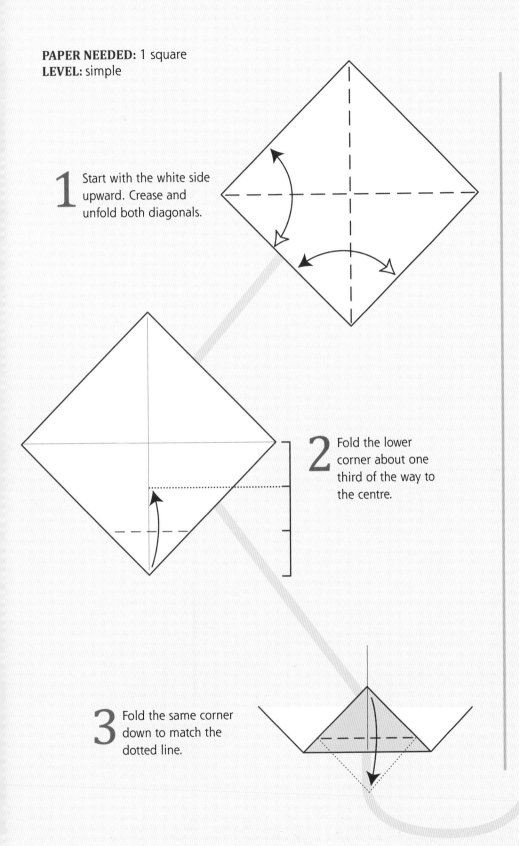

PAPER NEEDED: 1 square
LEVEL: simple

1 Start with the white side upward. Crease and unfold both diagonals.

2 Fold the lower corner about one third of the way to the centre.

3 Fold the same corner down to match the dotted line.

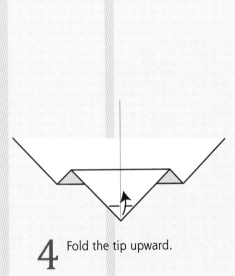

4 Fold the tip upward.

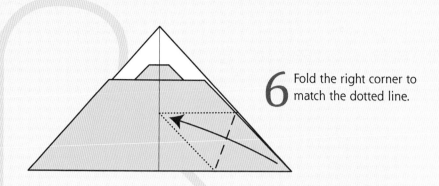

6 Fold the right corner to match the dotted line.

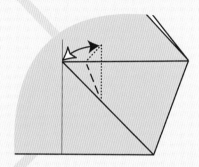

7 Fold the tip of the flap upward.

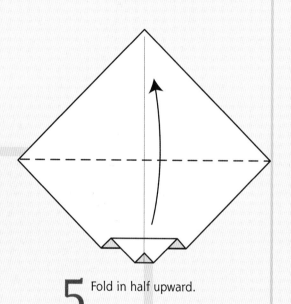

5 Fold in half upward.

8 Reverse this tip inside.

9 Unfold the lower half to the right underneath.

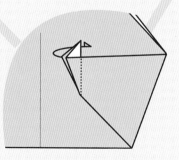

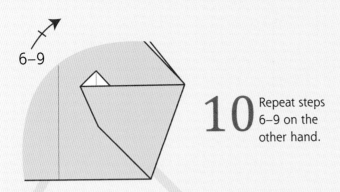

6-9

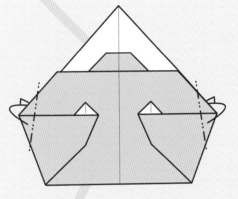

10 Repeat steps 6–9 on the other hand.

11 Fold the outer corners behind to round the model. Many variations are possible!

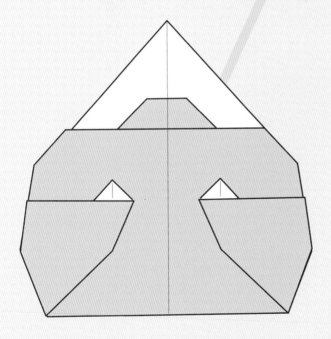

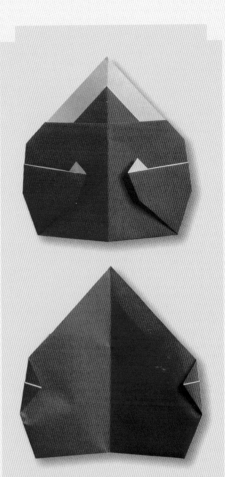

TIP: USING YOUR INSTINCT

As with many simple designs, a lot of the folding is "by eye"; in other words, you are not folding to a specific, marked location. The trick is to make a curved fold, then adjust it until you are happy with the result. Remember, there is no perfect shape – it's up to you! If you reinforce the vertical centre crease as a mountain, the model will stand.

Seated Buddha

This beautiful Buddha will give you pleasure both in its making and in its contemplation. Place it where you will see it often and be reminded of your diligent completion of a difficult task.

"In mindfulness of body be well fixed,
The monk restrained in the six spheres of sense,
Ever composed, could his nirvana know."

FROM THE UDANA (KHUDDAKA NIKAYA)

PAPER NEEDED: 1 square
LEVEL: intermediate

1 Start with the white side upward. Fold side to opposite side, crease and unfold, in both directions.

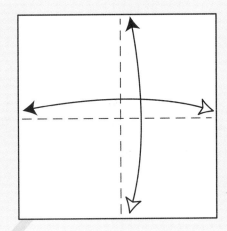

2 Fold the lower edge to the horizontal centre crease.

3 Fold the upper corners to the centre.

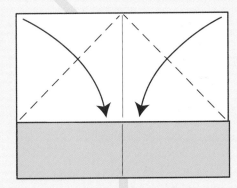

4 Fold the short left edge to the lower edge, crease and unfold. Repeat on the right. Turn the paper over.

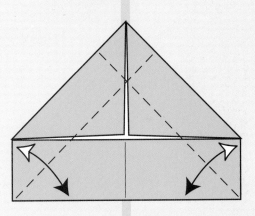

5 Fold the upper corner to the farthest crease intersection, crease and unfold.

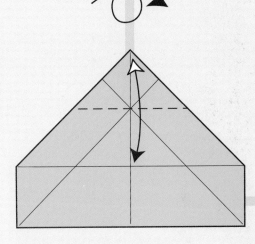

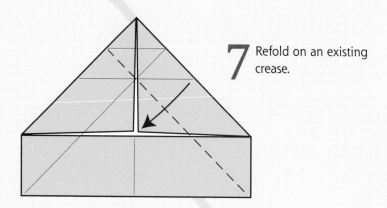

7 Refold on an existing crease.

6 Fold the upper corner to the nearest crease intersection, crease and unfold. Turn the paper over.

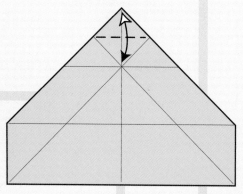

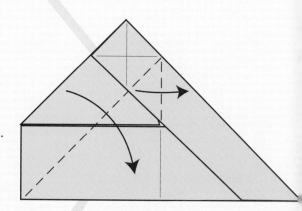

8 Fold the upper left edge inward, swivelling the top square around to the right.

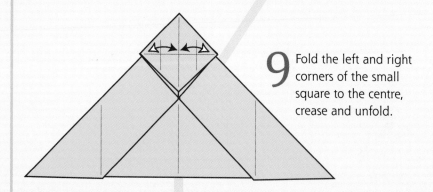

9 Fold the left and right corners of the small square to the centre, crease and unfold.

10 Change the upper creases to mountains, reversing the corners into the paper.

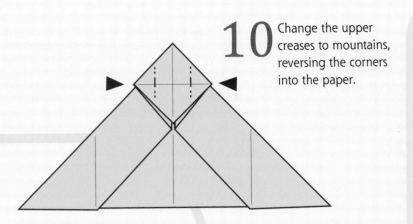

11 Fold the top corner behind on an existing crease, lifting up the lower corner.

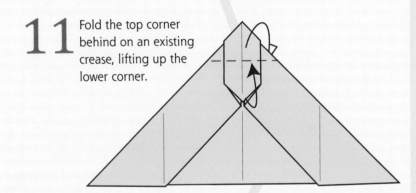

12 Fold the narrow flaps in half outward.

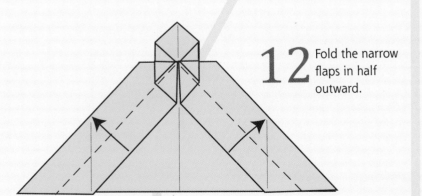

13 Fold over the tip of the upper flap. Turn the paper over.

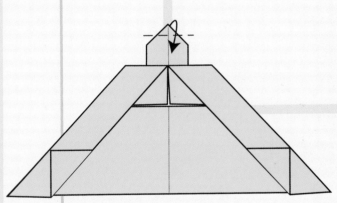

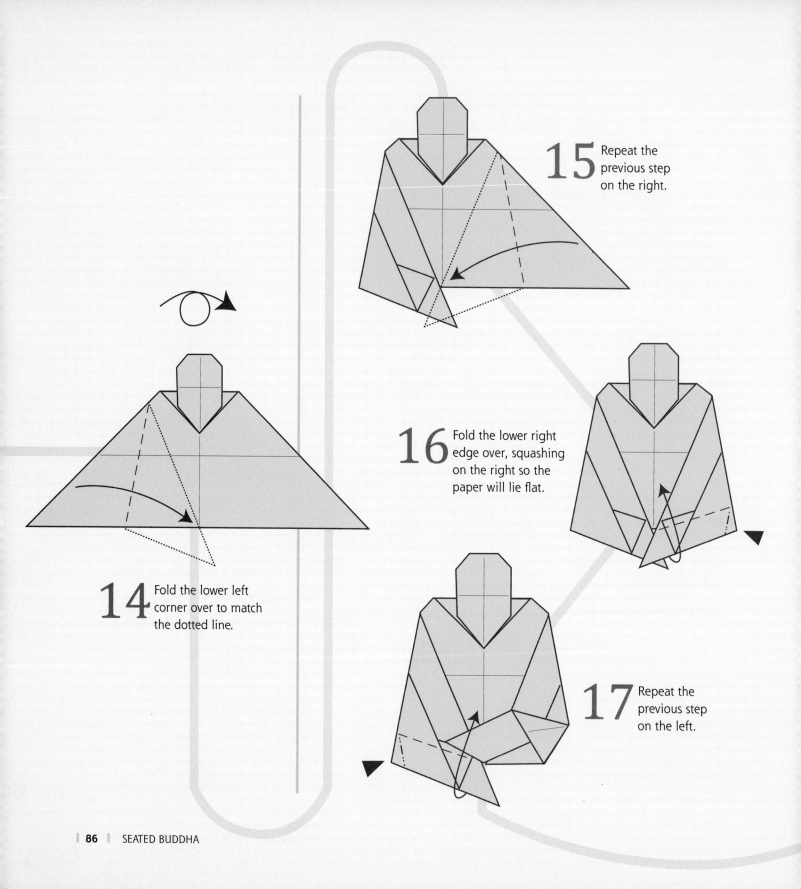

15 Repeat the previous step on the right.

16 Fold the lower right edge over, squashing on the right so the paper will lie flat.

14 Fold the lower left corner over to match the dotted line.

17 Repeat the previous step on the left.

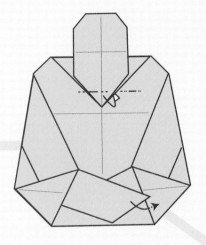

18 Fold the tip of the chin underneath. Tuck the point under a flap.

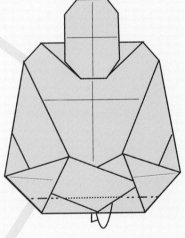

19 Fold the lower edge underneath, leaving the central flap as it is.

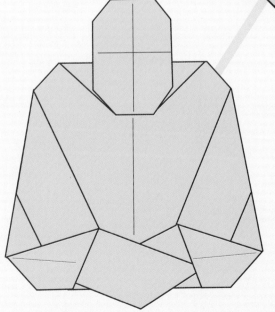

TIP: CAREFUL CREASING
Make the creases in step 9 very accurately, to help when the same corners are reverse-folded inside. Steps 16 and 17 are not located to specific points on the model. You need to judge "by eye" how large the sleeves will be.

Meditating Buddha

The Meditating Buddha is the trickiest project to master in this book. Staying calm and allowing the paper to help you as it takes form is the key to creating this beautiful and peaceful image.

*"Even if things don't unfold the way you
expected, don't be disheartened or give up.
One who continues to advance
will win in the end."*

DAISAKU IKEDA
(BUDDHIST LEADER AND POET, B. 1928)

PAPER NEEDED: 1 square
LEVEL: complex

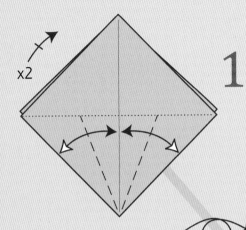

1 Start with step 6 of the Vase of Wealth (pages 33–4) rotated 180 degrees. Fold both lower edges to the vertical crease, but only in the lower half of the paper. Repeat on the two flaps underneath.

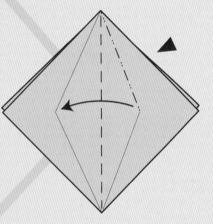

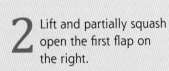

2 Lift and partially squash open the first flap on the right.

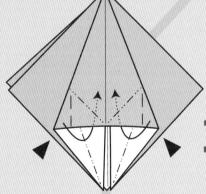

3 Fold the lower white edges inside, forming the mountain creases as you flatten the paper. Repeat on the left.

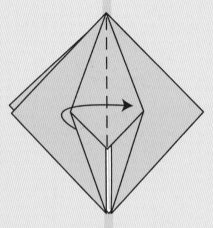

4 Fold the central flap in half to the right.

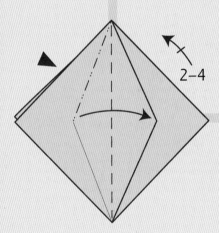

5 Repeat steps 2–4 on the first flap as a mirror image on the left.

6 This is the result. Repeat steps 2–5 on the underside.

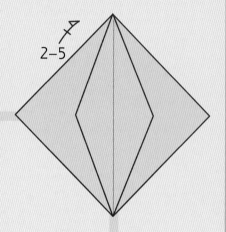

2–5

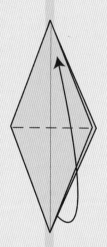

7 Fold the first flap at the bottom to the top.

8 Fold the triangular flaps up, then unfold.

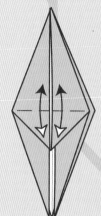

9 Pull the top flap upward, opening out paper and forming a mountain crease where the dotted line is – this will be vertical at the end of the step.

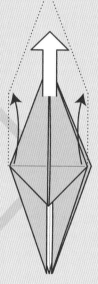

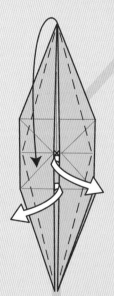

10 Pre-crease these valley creases individually, then fold the top corner to the bottom, opening layers on either side with the valley creases.

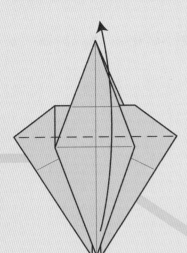

11 Fold a layer upward between the widest corners.

12 Fold the lower white layers to the centre, extending the creases into the upper half.

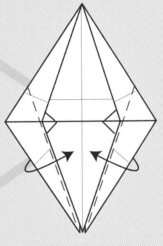

13 This is the result. Turn the paper over.

14 Fold two layers in half to the right.

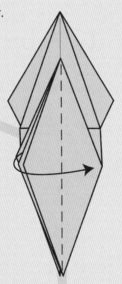

15 Fold a single corner from the bottom to the top.

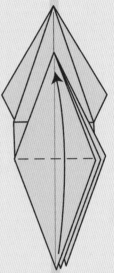

16 Fold back the first layer from the right, making a reverse fold with these creases to form the arm.

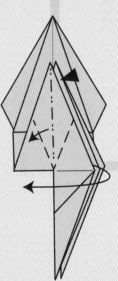

MEDITATING BUDDHA | **91** |

17 Fold in a corner from the left to the crease intersection.

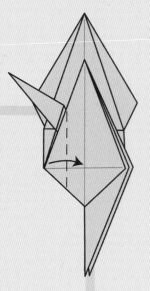

18 Ease out paper from inside the first flap.

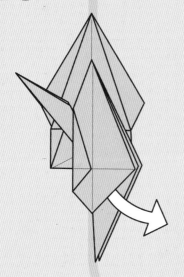

19 Fold a flap from the right to the left.

20 Repeat steps 14–19 on the right side.

14–19

21 Crease and unfold two vertical valley creases.

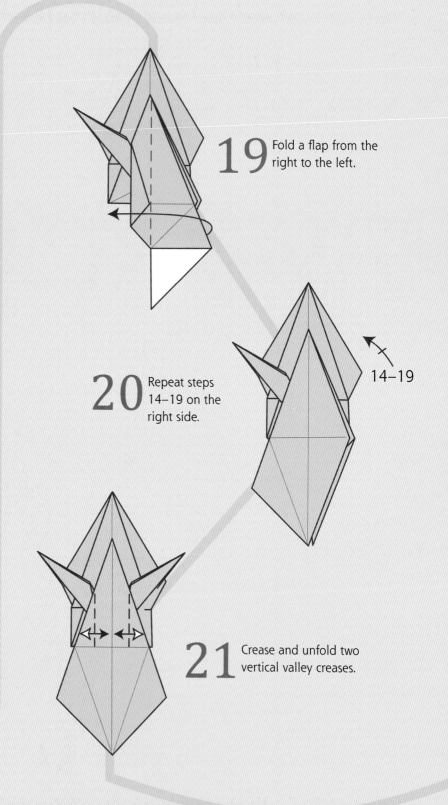

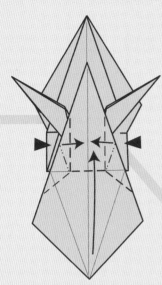

22 Use the same creases as you fold up the lower half, squashing the paper flat – see the next diagram.

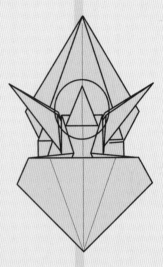

25 This is the result. Now we focus on the circled area.

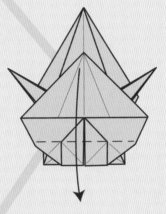

23 Fold the lower coloured section in half downward.

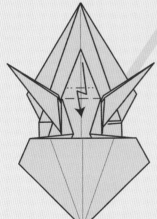

24 Make a pleat on the central triangular flap.

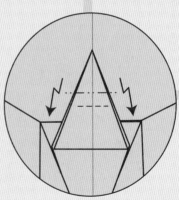

26 Make a similar pleat on the top of the flap.

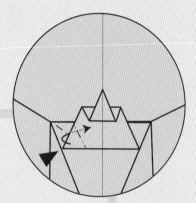

27 Reverse the corner inward to form the face.

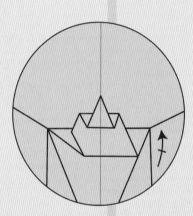

28 This is the result. Repeat on the right.

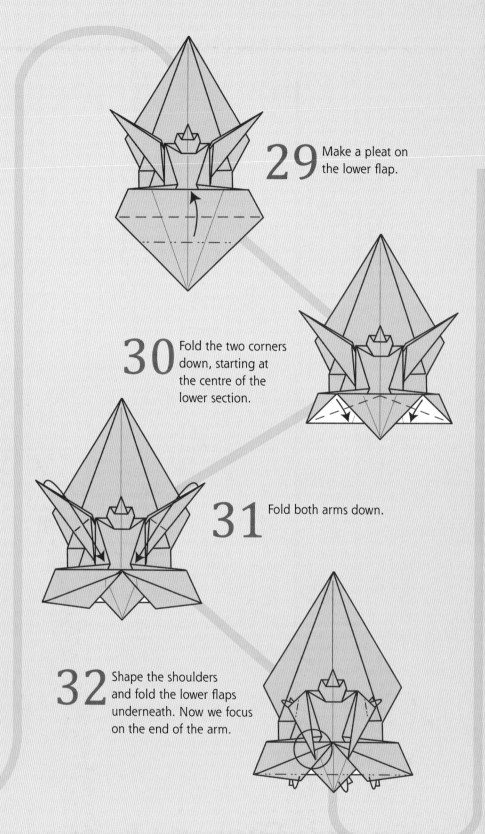

29 Make a pleat on the lower flap.

30 Fold the two corners down, starting at the centre of the lower section.

31 Fold both arms down.

32 Shape the shoulders and fold the lower flaps underneath. Now we focus on the end of the arm.

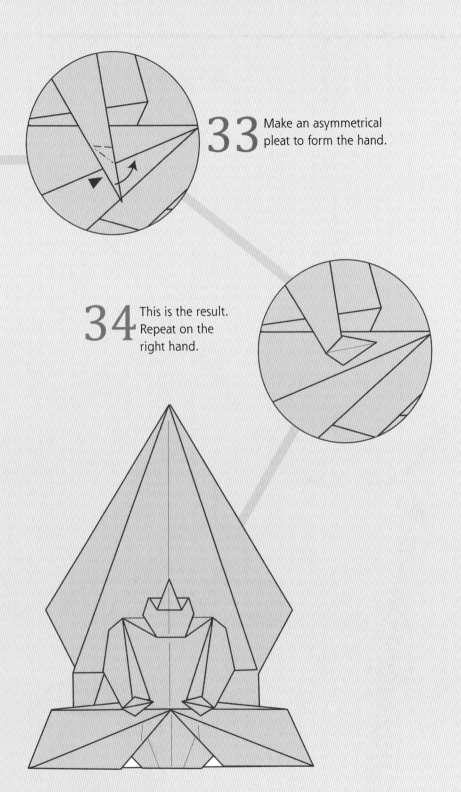

33 Make an asymmetrical pleat to form the hand.

34 This is the result. Repeat on the right hand.

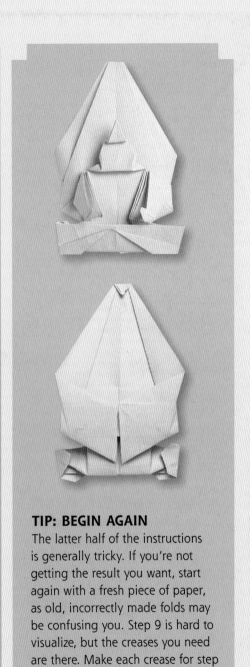

TIP: BEGIN AGAIN
The latter half of the instructions is generally tricky. If you're not getting the result you want, start again with a fresh piece of paper, as old, incorrectly made folds may be confusing you. Step 9 is hard to visualize, but the creases you need are there. Make each crease for step 10 individually before performing the step itself.

Taking it further

If you have enjoyed folding these models and wish to study origami further, there are many websites offering both diagrams and folding hints. You can find thousands of origami videos on the web, although not all are easy to follow! Most countries in the world have their own origami societies, with associated websites. Here are two of the oldest and best-established societies:

UK: www.britishorigami.info
USA: www.origamiusa.org

By joining one (or more!) of these groups, you will receive regular magazines packed with model diagrams, articles, photos of the latest designs and much more. You can also attend national conventions or conferences, organized almost everywhere in the world. There is also an electronic mailing list, which is free for anyone to subscribe to. The details are given here: lists.digitalorigami.com

Following diagrams on a screen is OK, but many people feel the best way to learn a model is from a book. Thirty years ago, you could have probably owned every origami book available. Nowadays, there are many thousands of books on offer, from simple to highly complex. Here are a few that will give you a lot to fold and to consider:

Origami Design Secrets by Robert Lang
Origami Omnibus by Kunihiko Kasahara
Roses, Origami & Math by Toshikazu Kawasaki
Origamido by Michael LaFosse
Spiral by Tomoko Fuse
Angel Origami by Nick Robinson

World's Best Origami by Nick Robinson
Eric Joisel – The Magician of Origami by Makoto Yamaguchi

Some of these books are not cheap, but well worth investing in. As a beginner, it is a good idea to buy an affordable book and fold your way through it for the experience.

Nick Robinson's website is at www.origami.me.uk

Design credits
The following models have been included by kind permission of the creators: Vase of Wealth (Saburo Kase); Foolish Monkey and Meditating Buddha (Kunihiko Kasahara); Wise Frog (Leyla Torres); Desk Buddha (Wayne Brown); Seated Buddha (Hanneke Van Der Kruit). Buddhist Wheel, Pagoda and Lotus of Peace are traditional designs. All other designs were created by the author.

Author acknowledgments
I would like to thank the creators listed above as well as the following: all the staff at Watkins Publishing for their help in bringing this project to life; Wayne Brown, who did a sterling job proofreading the diagrams; my (lucky) wife; my beautiful children for keeping my feet grounded; Ruby and Matilda (our moggies); plus all my friends in the British Origami Society and the wider international origami world, for their friendship and inspiration.